THE LAST

CHILDHOOD

THE LAST CHILDHOOD

A Family Story of Alzheimer's

CARRIE KNOWLES

THREE RIVERS PRESS
New York

Published by Three Rivers Press, New York, New York.
Member of the Crown Publishing Group.

Random House, Inc. New York, Toronto, London, Sydney, Auckland
www.randomhouse.com

Three Rivers Press is a registered trademark and the Three Rivers Press colophon is a trademark of Random House, Inc.

Originally published, in different form, as *Alzheimer's: The Last Childhood* by Research Triangle Publishing, Inc. in 1997. Copyright © 1997 by Carrie Knowles.

Book design by Susan Maksuta

Printed in the United States of America

Library of Congress Cataloging-in-Publication Data

Knowles, Carrie.
The last childhood : a family story of Alzheimer's / Carrie Knowles.—
1st Three Rivers Press ed.
Prev. ed. published as: Alzheimer's. Fuquay Varina, NC : Research
Triangle Pub., 1997.
Includes index.
1. Powers, Ruth Margaret—Mental health.   2. Alzheimer's disease—
Patients—Family relationships.   3. Alzheimer's disease—Patients—
Biography.   4. Aging parents—Family relationships.   I. Title.
RC523 .K64 2000
362.1'96831'0092—dc21
[B]
99-087346

ISBN 0-609-80648-3

10 9 8 7 6 5 4 3 2 1

First Three Rivers Press Edition

For my grandmother,
Laura Isabelle Barr.

My mother,
Ruth Margaret Powers.

And my sister,
Laura Ruth Mindel,
Who carries the names
Of her mother and grandmother
With dignity and spirit.
I feel lucky she is my sister.

ACKNOWLEDGMENTS

I would like to thank the North Carolina Arts Council for awarding me the Literary Nonfiction Writer's Project Grant that gave me the time to complete this work.

I would also like to thank my family for allowing me to tell this story. My children and husband for believing it was worth doing. Peggy Payne for the many lunches and fine friendship that has seen me through this project and others. Bonnie Tilson for support and guidance on the first book. Bernie Asbell for his insight and support. Regina Ryan, my agent, for bringing this book to Three Rivers Press. And to Sarah Silbert, who managed in her quiet way to make it better. Thank you.

CONTENTS

Contents

PROLOGUE

Last night I dreamed my mother knew my name. It was one of those dreams where you struggle all night to scramble up from the well of sleep into the real world so you can use the knowledge you've just gained to make things better. When I woke up, my first impulse was to get up, get dressed, go to the airport, fly to Michigan, and see if it was true. But of course, once I was awake and dressed, I knew that it had been a dream. If I went to Michigan, I would discover that my mother still had Alzheimer's and not only wouldn't know who I was but wouldn't know who she was either.

In my dream, I sat and talked to my mother. I pushed her in her wheelchair around the Methodist Home, and we looked out the windows. She introduced me to her friends. We had a fine visit. She showed me her right leg and told me where it hurt and how she had broken her hip when she fell. She explained to me, as we had explained to her, that she couldn't walk anymore because her brain and foot no longer talked to each other. I helped her into bed and propped her leg up on a pillow so she would be more comfortable. I looked for the doctor and asked if there were pain medicines he could give her. I called my sister and told her Mom knew my name and was our mother again.

In my dream, my sister and brothers were as delighted as I was to discover Mom was, except for her leg, fine. Mom thanked us for taking care of her and said she liked the Methodist Home. She said the people were good to her and her room was comfortable.

I remember crying in the dream when I told my mother I was sorry I had quit writing her. I confessed I had not written since I had last seen her because I had found all my cards and letters unopened in the drawer of her nightstand. This part of the dream was true. Though I had not made a conscious decision to quit writing her after finding my unopened letters, as Valentine's Day rolled by, I realized I had forgotten to send her my card. When I found the card a week later, I sat in my office and cried.

I was able to understand the part of the dream about not writing my mother, because it happened and I knew how it came to be in the dream. But I was shaken by the dream notion that we had failed to notice Mom was normal again. What gnawed at me all night long and into the next day was the idea that we had quit believing she would get better, so we had quit looking for her to get better. And maybe, just maybe, we were wrong and she had gotten better and we hadn't noticed.

It was one of those buried-alive dreams: a final-exam

nightmare where you have forgotten to take the class or can't find the door to get into the room. It was a failure dream. Somewhere deep inside myself, in the place where dreams come from, I believed I had failed my mother.

I am not the only one who feels this way. I know there are thousands of daughters, sons, and spouses who go to bed each night dreaming the kind of failure dreams I dream. I also know these family members go to sleep wondering what horrors the next day of Alzheimer's will bring them, because Alzheimer's is full of surprises, trials, and tribulations.

Left with no short-term or long-term memory, victims in the later stages of Alzheimer's cannot and do not talk about their disease. Therefore we have no way of knowing what they are experiencing.

The "other victims" of Alzheimer's, however, despite their good intentions and loving care, wrestle day and night with failure. The failure of overlooking the warning signs of the early stages of Alzheimer's. The failure to act quickly enough to keep the Alzheimer's victim from harm. The failure of not being able to make a difference or to stop the disease. The failure to remain memorable enough for their parent or loved one to recall. The failure to be a memory.

When our lives are so filled with memories, how could the lives of those we love be so empty of them?

I had another dream one night. In this dream, my mother looked the way she looks now, stooped and sunken and tired. We were visiting her, and after we had taken her for a walk outside to see the roses in the garden, she asked to be taken to her room. Go, she said, as we came to her room, let me get into bed. And then she said . . . If you would just go and take the children with you, I could sleep with your father again.

Our father has been dead since 1971. I called my sister to ask her what the dream meant. She said she didn't know. But of course we both knew that this was the "other" dream. The dream where you no longer believe things will miraculously get better, but instead you know how horrible the situation is, and you hope it will end. What you want in this other dream is not a miracle, but for your mother to go into a deep sweet sleep and slip away from this life to a place where she might find release and rest.

Both dreams carry the same wish: that your mother might find her life again.

These dreams and other real-life struggles are why I wrote this book. I hope it helps you think about what may be happening to you or someone you love. I hope my family's experiences help you make some sense out of what you are struggling with as your loved one slips farther and farther away from you. And I sincerely hope it helps you to know you are not alone in this nightmare. Most important, I hope this book makes you realize that you have not failed. You have done your best—the best anyone can do under these strange and powerfully disturbing circumstances.

THE LAST
CHILDHOOD

INTRODUCTION

Alzheimer's begins with the loss of short-term memory, progresses through the loss of not only fine and gross motor skills but involuntary motor skills as well, and ends when the victim is incontinent, incoherent, and bedridden. In the end, an Alzheimer's victim is unable to reflexively swallow their own saliva when they sleep, so they drown.

Discovering that Alzheimer's is a terminal illness is just one of the many shocks in store for family members of Alzheimer's victims. The other one is that from onset to death with Alzheimer's is, on average, seventeen years.

The long slow progression of the disease is disturbing, but more disturbing than that is the realization that you and your family either ignored or failed to notice what was going on during the early signs of the disease.

The signs are subtle.

You're out to lunch with your mother, and she fidgets with the menu. It's a restaurant you've been to together a dozen times before. You ask her what she's going to have, and she gets agitated. She says everything costs too much. You tell her you're paying the bill and not to worry. She calls the waiter over and makes a scene over the price of the food. This is one of a dozen such scenes about money and bills you have witnessed over the past year. You're embarrassed about the scene but also worried that something is wrong with your mother. You don't ask her what's wrong because you're not quite sure how to ask such a question. Instead, you apologize to the waiter and try to calm your mother. When you pay the bill, you leave a generous tip and make a mental note not to come back here with her again.

A few weeks later, she isn't ready when you go to take her out shopping, even though you called the night before to let her know when you'd be coming. You remind her you called, and she gets agitated. She says you didn't call. You say you did. You have an argument about it, then leave wondering what happened.

What is happening? It could be nothing, just a bit of frustration and agitation over the spiraling costs of living and a touch of forgetfulness. It could also be the early signs of Alzheimer's. It's hard to tell the difference. Although the scene over the price of the meal and the argument over whether you called makes you feel like something might be wrong, you don't know for sure. Also, you're a little uncomfortable "jumping to the conclusion" that these incidences mean your mother has some form of dementia such as Alzheimer's. You don't want to sound like an alarmist. Besides, nobody wants to believe their parent or their loved one has dementia.

After my book, *Alzheimer's: The Last Childhood*, first came out in 1997, Dr. Webster Ross, a medical researcher with the Hawaii Center for Health Research in Honolulu, Hawaii, published an article in the *Journal of the American Medical Association* entitled "The Failure of Family Members to Recognize the Early Stages of Alzheimer's." Dr. Ross's research showed that it takes most family members five to seven years to recognize the early signs of Alzheimer's.

There are, of course, exceptions to this rule. Individuals in their forties who show signs of the early stages of Alzheimer's are more likely to be recognized by their families and friends as having something wrong with them than those in their late sixties or seventies. Therefore younger people are more likely to be diagnosed earlier. Why? Because someone who is forty or fifty is more likely to be depended upon by others, so when they begin to fail to fulfill their daily obligations, their failures are noticed. An office manager's mistake or a mother's failure to pay bills, cook meals, or care for her children is hard to miss. Forgotten bills and appointments, mistakes, and failures to perform simple tasks are more likely to go unnoticed when fewer people are depending on that person or are paying attention to what they are doing.

Some exceptional families realize early on that the forgotten phone call, the missed appointment, and/or the obsessive concern about details or money signals that something is organically wrong, and they look for help. But these, as Dr. Ross's research and my personal experiences show, are the rare exception.

Since *Alzheimer's: The Last Childhood* first came out, I have been traveling around the country talking to family members who are struggling with Alzheimer's. What I have found is not families who knew, but families who are stunned that they didn't realize or recognize those early incidents as beginning signs of dementia. Those who did suspect that something might be wrong had difficulty convincing their siblings that they should seek help. So instead of taking action, they gave up and waited to see if things got worse. These families are not so much in denial, although there is some of that, as they are in shock. They are in shock that it is happening in their families; they are stunned that they are now responsible for caring for this person; and they are surprised that they had failed to notice or do anything until a crisis occurred.

It takes from five to seven years for family members to recognize the early signs of Alzheimer's. How can something that big and awful escape notice for so long? First, family members often fail to figure it out because they are afraid to know. It is the scary side of denial. If you *know* and acknowledge you know, then you have to take responsibility for it. You have to fix it.

Secondly, Alzheimer's is a disease with no easily measurable presenting symptoms. Unlike other illnesses, there is no fever, no change in blood pressure, no infection that can be measured by counting white blood cells, no stomach or headache, no cut that doesn't heal, no persistent cough, no dizziness, no nausea, no swelling or unusual growth, no slurred speech. In fact, during the early stages, there are no apparent physical changes at all that we've come to expect with disease. The body seems well. In fact, the body looks, walks, and talks like it is normal, except for the occasional memory slip or odd behavior.

Unfortunately, the most reliable "test" for Alzheimer's is observation. Which means that if we don't know what to look for, we can't understand what we are seeing. Also, if we are not around the person in question, we can't observe the subtle changes taking place. In addition, there's more to just seeing in observing. With Alzheimer's, it's important to trust your gut feelings that something is wrong with the person you love, and you need to act on it.

Fortunately there are now some guidelines to help us. When the National Hospice Association made the decision to offer respite care to family members, it structured its care provision as it had with cancer: to provide care in the "last stages" of the disease. Which led it to look for some system to help assess where the Alzheimer's victim was, along the continuum of the disease, and when the association might need to step in to help.

What they chose was the Functional Assessment

Staging (FAST) evaluation system, developed by Dr. Barry Reisberg. FAST looks at the various symptoms and manifestations of the disease, from forgetfulness to an inability to perform complex tasks, incontinence, loss of language, loss of ability to walk, loss of ability to smile, and in the end, loss of the ability to hold the head up independently. Although Alzheimer's often affects people in unique ways, the progression from loss of short-term memory to loss of long-term memory, from loss of fine motor skills to loss of gross motor skills, is pretty universal. There are circumstances, such as a stroke, history of alcoholism, or the development of other diseases that may alter this course slightly or speed up the progression of the disease, but these are the exceptions rather than the rule.

FAST divides or categorizes the development of the disease into five stages: Incipient or Questionable Alzheimer's Disease (AD); Mild AD; Moderate AD; Moderate–Severe AD; and Severe AD. The first stage, the incipient or questionable stage, spans the first seven years of the disease. In this stage, the victim may complain about experiencing forgetfulness while exhibiting decreased job functioning as well as difficulty in traveling to new locations and in organizing their lives. This is the same seven-year period that Dr. Ross noted as the time when families fail to notice something is developing.

This book unfolds along the continuum of FAST, using my family's experiences to illustrate the various stages. Along the way, I've tried to raise issues confronting family members regarding their role in providing care for the Alzheimer's victim.

It would probably be helpful to know something about my family. We are four siblings: two girls and two boys, all born roughly five years apart. Our parents adopted my older brother, Gary, born 1945, when he was six weeks old. He's part Navajo Indian, and when they offered to find his birth mother when he was sixteen, Gary told Mom that as far as he was concerned, she was his mother, and we were his family, period.

He went to high school, graduated, joined the navy, and served a four-year tour aboardship in the Mediterranean (missing Vietnam by some stroke of good luck). He married his high school girlfriend when he was still in the service. He and his first wife, Pat, had one child, a boy, Danny. Nineteen years later, after twelve years of being foster parents, they adopted their second son, when he was three months old. He is now twelve. When Jamie became part of our family, we felt like life had come full circle: our father was adopted, Gary was adopted and now, he had adopted a son. Jamie and our father, coincidentally, share the same birthday.

My sister Lolly married her high school sweetheart, Thomas Mindel. Thomas has been with General Motors since he graduated from high school and is a skilled trades specialist in hydraulic pipe fitting. Lolly stayed close to home, attended a local community college, and has worked on and off for the past fifteen years as a designer and typesetter for various publishing concerns. They have two sons, Quentin and Colin.

My younger brother, Chuck, attended college but stopped short of graduating. For many years, he held a string of odd jobs that allowed him to piece together a part-time life as a musician. He recently found a new career, ironically as a corporate headhunter, and is settling down into the struggling middle class. He still plays trombone and sings; likes big-band music, rhythm and blues, and country grunge; has gigs on occasion; and now earns enough money to pursue his second love, scuba diving. He was engaged once but broke the engagement right before the wedding. He was struggling at that point in his life with our mother and also with career options. His fiancée left him because she decided she wanted a "professional" man for a husband. He has since met the love of his life, and the two of them live together and travel around on their sailboat.

I am the second child. I went to college and delayed getting married until I was thirty, when I had the good fortune of meeting and falling in love with Jeff Leiter. Like many women in that same life-loop I found myself needing to make decisions about having children at the "height" of my career. When our first son, Neil, was born, Jeff was thirty-three and I was thirty-two. I was thirty-six when Hedy came and forty-one when our son Cole arrived.

Our father, Paul Knowles, was blind since birth. He was thirteen years older than Mom. He died a few weeks after I graduated from college. Gary was married by then, Lolly was in high school, and Chuck was eleven. Mom remarried a few years later to a divorcé with no children. His name was Ray Powers. Mom met Ray while continuing our father's work with Leader Dogs, a guide-dog agency for the blind, and the Lions Clubs International. Ray was also blind. When Mom and Ray married, Chuck was the only one living at home.

For the most part, since leaving school, we have all been independent from Mom. Two of us live out of state and two in state. And we all, except Chuck, have young children at home.

We live fairly simple lives. We work. We try to take good care of our children, and like hundreds of thousands of middle-class, middle-aged people today, we also take care of Mom.

At the moment, our mother remains physically well while she declines mentally. It is not always clear what she needs from us. Sometimes she just needs for us to sit with her. Other times she wants us to "go."

Her disease has taken a toll on our lives. We have felt the pressure of the constant stress of her deterioration. We have all become acutely aware of how short and precarious life can be. My older brother Gary left his first wife after many years of being in a difficult marriage. He has since remarried and claimed a new life for himself.

Lolly left her job and decided she would take a chance and try the thing she has most wanted to do in her life: raise and train horses. She now cleans stalls and grooms horses in exchange for board for her mare and colt while she's learning to train. Chuck and his delightful companion Margi are taking a year off from their jobs to sail wherever the wind takes them.

As for me, I have recently undergone reconstructive kidney surgery to correct a congenital defect that had previously been undetected but had, over the years, caused serious damage to my kidney. Why did I discover this problem now instead of twenty years ago? Some would argue the stress of my life put stress on my kidney, causing the defect to manifest itself.

I cannot deny I have been under a great deal of stress over the course of my mother's illness. And I know the stress has done damage, but it has also done some good. I have learned through helping my sister care for our mother that you can take on too much, and too much is no good for anyone.

I pay more attention to my family now and try to make our time together as good as it can be. We take "time off" and travel together. I have also given up a number of committees I used to serve on, and I never agree to do anything without saying I have to think about it or look at my calendar first. I give myself a day to think it through, and if it feels right and I believe I can manage it without adding more stress to my life, I say yes. If it doesn't, I turn it down.

Like my brothers and sister, over these years with Mom, I have also done something good for myself. I learned how to throw pottery. I have no ambitions for my pottery. It's my mud therapy. It keeps me sane.

Lolly's life, more than the rest of ours, is occupied with Mom's day-to-day care. Her days are filled with papers, checks, lawyers, and reports, as well as care conferences and sewing labels in Mom's clothing. As legal guardian, Mom occupies her time and attention. The horses give her something that is just hers, and through them she is able to carry on being the one in charge of Mom without "stressing out" too badly.

We have all read the studies that show there may be a genetic component to Alzheimer's, and we have read the ones that say genetics is less of a factor than aging. We worry about the fact that we may be likely to get the disease either because of Mom or because we will live long enough to develop it, but we try hard not to think about it. If you think about it too much, it will drive you crazy.

Taking care of Mom is a lot like taking care of a strong-willed child. I had not known about FAST when I named this book. In light of FAST, however, the title I chose, *The Last Childhood*, is more appropriate than I had first realized. As the disease progresses, the victim does in fact become more and more like a child. So the caregiver has to take on not only the care of someone who is sick but also the role of parent. Ironically, when we think of parenting, of raising a child to adulthood, we are looking at the same span of seventeen years.

When I tell someone about FAST and the seventeen years, I can see them counting on their fingers, trying to construct their own time line. Everyone wants to believe they are nearing the end. "My mother isn't doing this," they tell me, "but she is doing that." "She's in the last stage, isn't she?" they ask. I tell them I don't know. I'm not a doctor. I tell them that the end, like the beginning, is a slow-moving, painful process. It feels never-ending. I tell them they need to look for help, for ways to make new memories for themselves and for their families so they will not be caught up in the drowning pool of this slow dying.

Our family, like the families in Dr. Ross's study, did not see what was going on for a long time. We made a lot of mistakes. We are willing to share those mistakes in the hope that you and your family will be able to see yourselves in our shoes and act sooner. We also hope our mistakes, our fumbling for the right thing to do, and my mother's feisty, difficult progression through Alzheimer's will give you some hope, some sense that you are not alone in your struggle to care for someone you love.

1

QUESTIONABLE ALZHEIMER'S: THE EARLY STAGES

It is hard to pinpoint the moment Mom's Alzheimer's began. Whenever the siblings get together, we try to remember what happened when. We dig further and further into the past hoping to recall some incident that we can hold fast as the turning point. It is an exercise meant to bring clarity to our collective history.

There is no single moment that any of us can point to and say, There, that's when it started. We do know now, however, from her checkbook and her financial records, that things were beginning to go wrong for a long time before we could see it. In retrospect, when we were given access to her financial records, we realized that just about the same time her financial records became erratic, so did her behavior.

When we were living through those erratic times, we

shrugged them off as quirky emotional swings. We often described them as "just Mom" or maybe a case of "nerves." Mom had always been a bit high strung, and her mood swings were nothing new to us. Her early erratic emotional swings, irrational behavior, and explosions of anger seemed at the time to be less warning signs that something was wrong than isolated episodes that could be explained by aging and extenuating circumstances. There were a number of times over those years when we remarked on her behavior and asked what was wrong, but our questions were always met with anger, so we quit asking.

One incident early on, however, should have cued us in to the possibility that something was organically wrong. My siblings' families and mine were invited to come to Mom's for Thanksgiving in 1985. When we arrived, we discovered her oven door had fallen off. When we asked her when it had happened, she said she couldn't remember, maybe sometime back in August. When we offered to call a repairman or to go out and get the parts to fix it ourselves, she became agitated. She refused the repairs, saying there was really nothing wrong with it, and all we needed to do to cook the turkey was tie the door on. We persisted, she became angry, and in the end, we did as she said and tied the door on with a rope. Each time we basted the turkey, we had to untie the door. It took three of us to baste the turkey: one to untie the rope, one to hold the door, and one to do the basting. Each time we did it, it seemed weirder and weirder. We laughed about it once, but not a second time, because the explosion of anger that our laughter brought from Mom let us know this was no laughing matter. Little did we understand then just how unlaughable the situation was or would be in the future.

That same winter Mom realized she and Ray had feathered a rather healthy nest egg at the bank. After adding the figures together, she called me one afternoon to say she was going to go to the bank to pay off her mortgage. I knew she had ten years left on the mortgage and that paying it off would wipe out more than half of their savings. I tried to talk her out of it because they had a fairly low interest rate and an easy mortgage payment, even on their limited income. Also, I knew if something serious happened to either of them and they needed extended medical care, the only thing they had to fall back on was their savings. If she wiped out half of it, they could be in trouble.

By then, Ray had been sick off and on with little things that signaled big trouble coming: a couple melanomas removed from his face and back, some persistent bladder problems, an erratic heartbeat, and high blood pressure. I urged her to keep her money in the bank and to keep plugging away at the mortgage.

She got angry. She told me I didn't know anything about finances. Then she hung up the phone, marched to the bank, withdrew the money, and paid off the mortgage. What my mother did with her money was her business, so I forgot about it.

Then one day in the spring of 1986, Mom called me. A lifelong friend of hers had refused to run an errand for her that morning because she was too busy with her own errands, although she offered to run it for her later. My mother was furious with her and seemed, to me, to be completely out of control. When I suggested she should call her friend and talk about it, she hung up the phone.

A few days later, Mom sent me a photocopy of the letter she had written to her friend saying she never wanted to hear from her again. The letter made my stomach churn and my head spin. I couldn't believe my mother had written it. It was so ugly and mean-spirited, it made me think for a moment that I really didn't know my mother at all. I called the woman's daughter and explained that I didn't think Mom meant what she had written, and I added that we believed Mom hadn't been herself lately. I asked my friend to please talk with her mother and tell her to throw the letter away and not read it.

My brothers and sister would call each other when other things like the letter happened, and we would talk about what was going on. Ironically, it made us feel like children again: powerless. At the end of every conversation, we'd all agree that there was nothing we could do. In truth, there wasn't one of us who had the nerve to try to stand up to Mom and tell her she was wrong. Her reactions were so fierce and angry during this time that just the thought of the onslaught that might ensue if we questioned her behavior stopped the four of us from taking any action. Instead, we all hoped and prayed that whatever was wrong with her would just go away.

Looking back, I think that we, as her family, were irresponsible in our inaction. The story about the oven door is funny, but the one about her best friend is not. When I told someone the story about the letter, they looked at me in surprise and asked why I didn't immediately take my mother to a shrink.

Easier said than done. When was the last time you tried to tell your mother or father you thought they were crazy and needed psychiatric attention? Also, early Alzheimer's behaviors are so erratic and irrational, they kind of take you by surprise. In addition, children are conditioned to believe their parents are right. The result of this early conditioning is to question your own sanity and not your mother's when something bizarre occurs. During her early stages of Alzheimer's, we spent a lot of time trying to figure out who was right, who was wrong, and who was crazy.

We did, in fact, try several times over the next couple of years to get Mom to a doctor. With an Alzheimer's victim, this rather simple solution is much harder to implement than you could possibly imagine. First you must remember that we weren't at all sure she had Alzheimer's. Our own family doctor, when we described her behavior, suggested it might not be Alzheimer's at all but a vitamin deficiency, the result of a small stroke, or perhaps even a brain tumor. As you can well imagine, if Mom was unwilling to talk about getting her oven door repaired, she was *definitely* not willing to talk about whether she was eating right and taking her vitamins, much less whether her "crazy" behavior was a result of a brain tumor.

There was nothing wrong with her, as far as she was concerned. Quite the contrary: If there was anything wrong, it was with us. We didn't press the point. Any suggestion that she might need to see a doctor brought on a terrifying avalanche of anger.

So instead of forcing the issue and braving the anger, we waited. We waited to see if the trouble would pass. We waited to see if she would take action on her own. We wondered if she might have a vitamin deficiency. We hoped she was just in a funk or having a long string of bad days. And we waited to see if she would get worse.

At about this same time, one of my mother's younger sisters, Aunt Geneva, was diagnosed as having Alzheimer's. Our cousin Robyn, Geneva's youngest daughter, and my cousin Brenda's sister, has told us she has a clear moment she holds in her mind as the beginning of her mother's disease.

Aunt Geneva used to take care of Brenda's children. At the time, Brenda lived next door to her mother. Brenda is the principal of the elementary school in their town. One day when Geneva was over at Brenda's house watching her children, Geneva's house caught on fire.

There had been a terrible storm the night before, flooding the low-water bridge in the valley where they live, in the Ozarks of Missouri. Sometime around mid-morning, a neighbor who was driving by saw fire coming from Geneva's house. He knew Geneva was at Brenda's and went over to get her.

The neighbor brought Geneva and Brenda's children to the burning house. By then, smoke was curling up the chimney and pushing itself from beneath the closed windows and doors.

Everything Aunt Geneva owned was inside her house: antiques collected over many years, pictures from the family, pictures and possessions of Otto, her deceased husband, and everything of any worth she had ever held in her life. The neighbor went into the house and retrieved a metal file box with valuable papers and photos just inside the bedroom door, but he held Geneva back because of all the smoke.

It was raining, but the rain didn't seem to touch the fire. With the bridge flooded, there was no way for the fire truck to get into the valley to put out the fire. There was no way to stop what was happening.

Geneva wouldn't budge from the scene. She stood out in the rain watching the slow-burning fire darken the windows and peel the white paint from the clapboard siding. Brenda was called and came home from school. She wrapped a blanket around her mother's shoulders and took her back to her own house to sleep.

For Robyn and Brenda, the fire was a clear starting point. The whole event, the fire, losing everything, then their mother having to rebuild her home and refurnish her life, was important. The disruption to Aunt Geneva's life and the many decisions that Aunt Geneva was confronted with after the fire allowed Robyn and her siblings some insight. They were able to see the changes resulting from the early stages of Alzheimer's more clearly and within a shorter time frame than they would have if the fire hadn't occurred. As Robyn explained, "At first she seemed fine, or at least no different than she had always been before the fire, but within a year we feared something was wrong."

For us, it was less clear cut. We had those incidents of truly unusual behavior, but the day-to-day indicators were very subtle. During the years between 1985 and 1990, though, we became more and more aware that Mom was no longer safe behind the wheel of a car. She clearly suffered from impaired judgment, as well as slower reflexes and a tendency to get flustered and angry when confronted with a complex series of tasks. Translation: We knew she shouldn't drive because driving is, in fact, a complicated orchestration of hands, feet, eyes, brain, and reflexes.

The car, however, was more than transportation for Mom. It was a badge of independence as well as interdependence. When our father was alive, Mom used to drive all over the country with him, taking him from one speaking engagement for Leader Dogs to another. Every summer on May 30, we would pack up the car and "go on the road" with Dad, arriving back on September 1 for school. Mom not only drove solo during all this time, she drove, for the most part, without maps. She had an amazing mind, and once she drove a route, she never forgot it. She knew every highway and shortcut from the East Coast through the Midwest. Driving was a sport, her sport, and she was clearly one of the best.

Our stepfather, like our father, was blind. This meant that once again Mom was the sole driver of the family. If Ray was aware of Mom's increasing inability to drive safely, he didn't let on. His lack of response or concern, however, didn't surprise us, because he rarely spoke to any of us about anything. When we suggested, out of concern for both of them, that Mom should stop driving and they should start taking cabs instead, both of them got angry with us and dismissed the notion without discussion.

Despite their refusal to consider taking cabs, Lolly was getting more concerned as time rolled on. When I came to visit in the spring of 1986, Lolly suggested I go shopping with Mom so I could see for myself if she should or should not be driving anymore. I understood Lolly's desire to get some confirmation about what was going on, so I agreed and arranged a shopping trip.

At the time, Mom was sixty-six years old and was concerned about being able to pass her next driver's test coming up in the fall. It was no trouble getting her to drive, because she was feeling defensive about her driving and wanted to show me how well she was doing behind the wheel for "an old bird of sixty-some."

Despite her earlier bravado, she was a little nervous as she drove and repeatedly cursed at the other motorists, whom she felt had encroached on her territory. She honked her horn and shouted out the window. Other than occasionally becoming totally enraged at someone for doing something stupid and calling them a "piss-ant," my mother's official oath, I never remembered her swearing in public or in private before this shopping trip. It took me by surprise, but I laughed it off, trying to defuse the situation a little. She swore at me and told me to keep my mouth shut.

While driving to the shopping mall, she saw a shoe store and stopped. It was a shoe store I had never been to before in my life. As we pulled up to the front of the store, Mom started talking about all the pairs of shoes she had bought there for me and for my brothers and sister. I was dumbfounded, first by her profanity and anger, and then by her belief that we had been here before.

She insisted we go into the store. When we went inside, I told her again, I hadn't been there before. She laughed and took my hand and told me I just didn't remember. She introduced me to the salesperson: he was equally baffled. Holding my hand while talking to the salesperson, she babbled on and on about how many shoes we had bought there and where I was living now and what I was doing. She tried to buy me a pair of shoes that weren't my size, and when I told her they wouldn't fit, she got angry.

What's happening here? I thought to myself. Who's lost it? Have I done something wrong? Have I forgotten I have been here before? Has my mother always been like this?

My head was racing, and I was beginning to feel frightened. Something was terribly wrong with either my mother, with me, or with our relationship. Mom didn't want to leave the store. She kept talking to the salesman and looking at soft newborn-baby shoes, although no one had a little baby to buy shoes for right then. She kept finding things she wanted to buy, none of which fit her or anyone in our family. I began to realize we weren't going to be able to leave until something was purchased, so I quickly found a pair of shoes that fit me, gave the clerk my credit card, made a purchase, and got out of there.

Later on, when we had finished shopping in the mall, Mom started to pull out of the parking lot and became flustered. For some reason, she was determined that she was going to make only right-hand turns on the way home. The easiest exit was a left turn, but we proceeded to make an awkward and lengthy exit to the right, circling the entire mall, then taking a long, roundabout way home because she didn't want to make any left turns.

By the time we got home, my mother was sputtering

and spitting with anger because I had tried to point out to her that it would have been easier and shorter if we had only made a left turn or two. I was upset but totally convinced that Lolly was right: Mom shouldn't be behind the wheel of any car.

You cannot, however, get someone's license revoked because they refuse to make left-hand turns. Mom continued to drive and, to our way of thinking, get worse.

That summer we drove up to visit her. It was a very hot summer, and she complained repeatedly about the heat. Her house had no air-conditioning. In response to her complaints, my husband, Jeff, suggested she might want to think about installing central air-conditioning.

She became so enraged at his suggestion that she threw us out of her house, saying we were not welcome there anymore. When I tried to call her from the road to make sure she was all right, she said she didn't know who I was and hung up the phone.

For the next six months, whenever I called, which I did every week just as I had all my adult life, she pretended we had a bad connection and hung up.

After that, I became the target and brunt of Mom's anger. It was a horrible and difficult time for me. I went to see a therapist. When I told the therapist what had happened and how I felt, she told me my mother was an angry woman and that I had not recognized or accepted her anger before. She advised me to cut my emotional ties with my mother and get on with my life.

She was my mother. I couldn't. When I talked with my brothers and sister about the way Mom was treating me, we decided Mom must have been going through a difficult time with Ray. We never once thought she might be sick.

2

FROM MILD ALZHEIMER'S TO A CRISIS

By 1991, Mom's short-term memory loss was becoming quite noticeable. She'd forget appointments, forget what she'd told us, and forget we called. She'd even forget we were coming to visit. We also noticed that she didn't seem to be cooking much or cleaning house.

When we mentioned cooking or the house, she'd wave us off gruffly and tell us she didn't have time. Ray wasn't feeling well, she'd say, and we had no idea how much work it was just to take care of him.

We also began to worry more about her driving. She seemed easily distracted and flustered. The thought of her driving all over town was making us more and more nervous.

Ray was little or no help. When we asked him about her driving, he'd say it was none of our business. But we felt we needed to do something before one of them got killed. We didn't, however, know quite what to do to get the car away from her.

Then Lolly got what seemed like a great idea. Mom was due for an eye exam. Lolly knew she was beginning to have trouble with her left eye, so she decided to talk to the doctor and ask him to flunk Mom on her exam so we could then take the car away from her.

When it came time for Mom's exam, Lolly offered to schedule the appointment. She also said she'd drive, since Mom would not be able to see clearly once the doctor put drops in her eyes. When Lolly called to make the appointment, she told the doctor about our concerns and about her idea to get Mom from behind the wheel. She explained to the doctor that this would be easy for him to do since Mom had had double cataract surgery and poor night vision and peripheral vision and was complaining about losing more vision in her left eye. Lolly also pointed out to him that during Mom's last exam, he had informed Mom that she was legally blind in her left eye without corrective lenses.

When Mom had finished her exam, she came to Lolly in the waiting room beaming. She bragged she passed with flying colors.

As Mom was making her pronouncement, the doctor called Lolly into his office, shut the door, and began lecturing her on the fine points of growing old. He told Lolly she should be ashamed of herself for even considering taking the car away from Mom. He told her young people did not understand that a driver's license was a valuable piece of independence for someone growing older, and it should not be taken away.

A week later, Mom was driving through town, got into an intersection, became confused, and broadsided another car. No one was hurt, but they could have been. Both cars had to be towed away.

Mom was well known in her little town, both because of my father and his work with Leader Dogs, and because she ran FISH, a volunteer social service agency that coordinated the efforts of the local churches, fire departments, and police departments to help families in need. The policeman who came to the scene of the accident recognized Mom, took her to the station, and then called Lolly to come get her.

Fortunately, Mom was completely rattled by the accident and turned over the car mess to Lolly. Lolly wisely called the insurance company and told them that as far as we were concerned, the car was "totaled," and we wanted them to write us a check and take the car away.

By this time, money was a major issue for Mom. She was sure she didn't have enough, and she also didn't seem to understand the difference between ten dollars and ten thousand dollars. The check from the insurance company was less than a thousand dollars. Lolly cashed it and gave it to Mom in small bills. Mom kept it in her purse and just looked at it, counting it from time to time. The idea of going out, selecting a new car, paying for it, putting gas in it, and driving it home must have seemed like a monumental task. She never mentioned it again.

Shortly after the car accident, Ray was diagnosed with

colon cancer and had surgery. After he came home from the hospital, the hospital sent a home health nurse to their house to check up on him. They wanted to make sure his colostomy bag was being properly cared for.

Mom apparently said or did something unusual—we never found out precisely what—because the aide left and filed a report saying he believed Ray was in danger. So the hospital sent a social worker.

The social worker started asking questions, and Mom became angry. At some point in the confrontation, the social worker asked if there were any other family members she could talk to. Mom said no, that we were either dead or had moved away and she didn't know where we lived.

The social worker, taking what Mom said to be the truth, reported the situation to social services, and they sent an ambulance to remove Ray from the house. And since she reported that there were no other family members to care for Ray, the state took custody of him and placed him in the first nursing home they could find. Needless to say, it wasn't a good situation, either for Mom or for Ray.

The whole event was quite a circus. When the ambulance left with Ray, Mom called Lolly crying hysterically, saying she didn't know what had happened but that something was very bad and Lolly had to come quick. Unfortunately, the damage had been done, and there was nothing Lolly could do, short of going to court to regain custody of Ray, to fix the situation. When Lolly asked Mom why she had told the social worker we were either dead or had moved away and she didn't know where we were, she said it was because the woman had been asking nosy questions and our family was none of her business.

Mom was just that kind of an outspoken wild woman, so it wasn't hard to imagine either that she said it or that it wasn't that long of a shot from normal for her. But once Ray was out of the house and Mom was completely on her own, we began to see that things were more out of control for her than we had previously imagined.

A couple of weeks after Ray left, Mom began having delusions. Unfortunately, it took us a while to realize they were delusions.

The first clue came when Mom called Lolly to say Ray had been drinking. Ray, in the years we had known him, would on rare occasions have a beer. He might have had some wilder days when he was young and in the service or single, but while he was married to Mom, we had rarely seen him with a drink in his hand, much less drunk.

It is, however, quite possible for someone to fool you. So when the first calls came, Lolly was skeptical but shrugged it off. Ray was in the hospital, and Lolly questioned Mom about the feasibility of him getting drunk under full-time nursing care.

Mom persisted in her story and said the man in the bed

next to Ray's was "slipping alcohol to him." She also insinuated this might not be so unusual. There was a Ray, she insisted, we didn't know. None of us except Chuck had lived with him, so what she was saying was possible if not wholly plausible.

Shortly after the reported "drinking incident," Mom began accusing Ray of exposing himself to the nurses, masturbating in public, and finally having sex with a nurse on his bed while Mom watched.

Lolly went to the home to see what was going on. Unfortunately, the nursing staff confirmed that it was Mom, not Ray, who was out of control and acting inappropriately. Ray was completely bedridden by this time and was hooked up to IVs, a colostomy bag, and occasionally some form of heart monitor. The staff were at their wits' end. Mom had not only caused quite a scene by accusing the nursing staff of having sex with her husband, but she was also dangerous to Ray. She had tried on more than one occasion to unhook the IV and monitors and to mess with the colostomy bag. They didn't want Mom visiting, but they couldn't legally ban a spouse from the ward.

Mom was clearly out of control. And like many Alzheimer's victims, she was obsessed with sexual things and foul language.

The situation with Mom was deteriorating rapidly, but we had our hands full trying to gain legal custody of Ray so we could move him to a better nursing facility closer to

Lolly's. A few weeks after Lolly went to court to gain custody of Ray, but before we could get him moved, he died.

I was out of the country at the time. Jeff was on a sabbatical in France, but I flew home immediately and went to Michigan to help Lolly with Mom. Lolly was pregnant with Colin and was having trouble keeping her blood pressure under control. As a result of Ray's death, there were mountains of papers to fill out and file and much to do. Most of all, we had to decide what to do with Mom.

We made a quick decision to move Mom to Lolly's. By then, we were sure Mom had some form of dementia, most likely Alzheimer's, and we knew she couldn't be on her own.

It was clear that her mental capacities had deteriorated, and Ray's death had moved her into a new realm of dependence. In fact, as each sleepless night progressed, it was becoming quite clear to us that she could never live on her own again, unless we could find reliable, saintly, twenty-four-hour nursing service.

Along about midnight, as the song goes, Mom would be up prowling the house. She would be in an agitated state of half-sleep. She would go from room to room turning on lights and rousing people from their sleep. Once she succeeded in waking one of us, she would ask us where she was, and before we could answer, she would begin looking for something: a purse, some money, or Ray. If we told her Ray died, she'd ask another question as though we hadn't said anything. We are not sure even today if she realizes he is gone.

We thought the darkness raised her anxiety, so we put a night-light in her room. When that didn't work, we bought her a big flashlight. She then made her nightly prowls with the flashlight in hand, shining the light in our eyes as she flitted from room to room.

She also had delusions. She thought there were burglars in the house. She thought Ray was trying to wake her up. She thought someone was trying to get her. Some of her delusions were sexual. None of them were pleasant.

We knew from our experience with Ray that in order to take care of Mom, we were going to have to gain custody of her. Lolly had initiated the proceedings right before Ray died but had not as yet gone to court. Without legal custody, we could not have access to her bank accounts, safe-deposit box, and the like. In short, we didn't have a clear picture of her legal or financial situation and therefore didn't know what kind of care we were going to be able to afford.

Because we didn't have legal guardianship of Mom, we also found ourselves in a financially complicated situation when Ray died and we needed to pay for his funeral. We were carefully trying to untangle Ray's estate without upsetting Mom or infringing on her legal or financial business. But this was difficult since all their accounts and property were held jointly, including the safe-deposit box. We had no way to search for Ray's life insurance policy, which we needed to pay for the funeral.

When Lolly mentioned the situation to one of the social workers who was helping us with the guardianship proceedings with Mom, she suggested we ask Mom about the policy. She said we should ask her every day, the same way each time, whenever Mom had a lucid moment.

So we did. After a week or more of asking her where his insurance policy was, one day Mom looked at us and said, "I don't know why you two girls keep asking me about Ray's life insurance. You know he was Catholic."

Catholic? We couldn't imagine what in the world being Catholic had to do with life insurance, so we asked her. Her response took us by surprise: "Catholics don't believe in life insurance policies," she said, "so I canceled them."

In retrospect it was funny, a great story to tell. In reality it was stunning. Without looking further, we knew it was true. We knew that in some quirky moment, she had done just that: canceled both his and her life insurance policies.

We later located a notation in her records about an insurance company. When we contacted them, they confirmed her story. The policies Mom and Ray had carried for years had been canceled without much notice. They were not cashed in but canceled. When we tried to explain that Mom had not been in full control of her faculties when she did it, the officer of the insurance company who had helped us untangle what had happened just smiled and essentially said, "Tough."

In order to satisfy the courts that we were not trying to gain custody of Mom just to get her money, but instead to take care of her because she could no longer take care of herself, we had to have Mom tested. Lolly and I made arrangements to take Mom to the Turner Geriatric Clinic at the University of Michigan. They have an excellent reputation for working with Alzheimer's victims, and we felt they would be able not only to satisfy the courts but to answer our questions and concerns as well.

Mom was angry with us for taking her. She was also angry with all the doctors because they kept asking her "dumb" questions.

At one point while the doctor was testing her, trying to determine if Mom had any short- or long-term memory loss by showing her pictures, asking her questions, and having her try to duplicate puzzle patterns, he left the room for a moment to get something. Unfortunately, the doctor's questions and "games" had agitated her beyond reason. Once the doctor was out of the room, Mom took off all her clothes and stormed out into the hall shouting obscenities at the doctor and anyone else who came along.

We were sitting in the lobby waiting for her, when we heard this ranting and raging woman, spitting out a string of foul words, and knew it was Mom. We looked up, and there she was, with nothing on except her shoes. We called for a nurse, who grabbed a sheet from an examining room, and we wrapped her up, calmed her down, and got her dressed. Despite the craziness of her act, it accomplished what she wanted: it ended the testing.

After the dust settled and Mom was calmer, the doctor came out and told us Mom was a textbook case. He believed without reservation that what she was experiencing was Alzheimer's.

We had long talks with our children, who at the time ranged in age from one to ten, to explain that it really wasn't okay to use the language Grandma used. We told them she was having trouble with her brain and didn't know what she was doing. We told them they were not to repeat what Grandma said, and they weren't supposed to giggle when she said bad words or did strange things.

It is not easy to explain Alzheimer's to children. Most children have a clear notion of what a grandmother should be: cuddly, easy, kind, knowledgeable, loving, and fun. Their grandmother was falling apart while they watched. She periodically took off her clothes and swore. She didn't know where she was, who they were, or who she was, and she couldn't sit still. She was antsy, as the kids called it. She was edgy, aggressive, angry, and highly unpredictable. But she looked—and occasionally even acted and sounded—like their grandmother.

The car crash, the incident with the social worker, the

delusions about Ray drinking and having sex, and the testing episode felt like an avalanche. It was as if Mom fell from competent to incompetent overnight. But in truth, she had been incompetent for a long while—years, in fact—but we couldn't or wouldn't see it.

I don't know what our children think or remember about those frightening times with her, but the story they always giggle over when she isn't around is the night we ordered Chinese takeout. We were all sitting at Lolly's kitchen table, passing food around, and Mom was taking some of this and some of that. We had made a big salad to go with dinner, and as things were moving around the table, Mom was handed a bottle of French salad dressing. Before anyone could say anything or stop her, she opened the bottle and gleefully doused her whole plate, covering the fried rice, beef and broccoli, cashew chicken, egg roll, and stir-fried vegetables in salad dressing.

It is the least scary and least offensive thing she did during that time, and if it is the memory they cling to, I will be grateful.

The night wanderings were a nuisance but were manageable. We kept the doors locked and tried gently to steer Mom back to bed, or at least to the family room to sit on the couch and look at magazines while the rest of us slept.

There were many scary aspects about keeping her in one of our homes. One day when I was making dinner, Mom came into the kitchen and picked up a piece of raw chicken and started to eat it. One of us screamed and grabbed the chicken away from her. Mom was furious because we wouldn't let her eat it. She started screaming, saying we were horrible because we didn't want her to have anything to eat; at the same time we were struggling to get the chicken out of her hand. It was a combination wrestling and shouting match. We eventually got the chicken away from her, and she left the room crying. It was a horrible scene, and we were badly shaken by the realization that her brain could no longer differentiate between cooked and raw food, good things to eat and bad.

The kids couldn't understand what had happened, and we tried to explain to them as well as to her that we were trying to keep her from harming herself. They were scared by all the commotion. Mom was in a fury, and at that point we knew beyond a doubt that we couldn't keep her at home anymore. But we didn't as yet have legal custody, and therefore we couldn't move her to an assisted living facility.

Without legal guardianship, we could not assume Mom's affairs. We could not use money from her accounts, and we could not force her to seek professional help. We also knew it was a complicated legal move to assume guardianship of a parent, since we had already tried that with Ray. Each state has different guidelines, and each judge has the right to interpret those guidelines.

Because neither Ray nor Mom had given us Durable

Power of Attorney (regular Power of Attorney does not allow you to make full financial and medical decisions for someone) over them, the only way we could gain control over their financial affairs in order to take care of them was to file for legal guardianship. When Lolly went to court to gain guardianship of Ray, it went smoothly. When her lawyer called her to give her a court date for Mom, he told her to brace herself. The judge she had drawn was known for being really tough on parent/guardianship cases. She needed to be prepared.

Lolly was nearing the end of her pregnancy and was exhausted. When she took the stand, the judge kept her for nearly an hour, grilling her on why she wanted guardianship. Finally, nearing the end of his examination of her, he asked her for her thoughts and beliefs about euthanasia.

The question stopped her cold. "Gosh," she said, "I haven't thought about it." The judge was silent. "I would have to give it a lot of thought," Lolly went on, not knowing what else to say but knowing we had to have guardianship of Mom. "Euthanasia is a rather serious situation." The judge seemed satisfied with her answer.

Later, as Lolly was leaving the courtroom, two men in suits who had been sitting in the back of the courtroom approached her. They were two lawyers hired by the state to examine Mom and proceed, if necessary, with state guardianship. They told her they had come on their own to give Lolly support if she needed it. They knew the judge and were aware of his reluctance to grant guardianship to children. They were also aware, after talking briefly with Mom a few months earlier, that hers was a clear case where guardianship was not only warranted but the best solution. They believed granting us guardianship was preferable to the state assuming the rights. If the judge had given Lolly more trouble, they told her, they would have stepped in and testified on her behalf.

What would have happened if we had tried five years earlier to assume legal and financial responsibility for Mom and her estate? In retrospect, if we had known then what we know now, maybe we would have tried. I believe, however, that because Mom was lucid then, "handled" her own affairs, and walked, talked, and looked "normal" most of the time, we probably would have lost. And in losing, we would have also damaged our future credibility with the courts.

At that time, judges, attorneys, and even doctors did not have any clear, well-defined guidelines or even "stages" of Alzheimer's. Even today there are many judges, lawyers, and doctors who are unaware of the various stages in the long course of Alzheimer's. There is still, unfortunately, no definitive road map of what to do and expect when living with an Alzheimer's victim. Each Alzheimer's victim seems to follow their own individual course through the disease, making every step of the way an experiment by trial and error: a veritable minefield of new and difficult experiences. But however differently the disease presents and progresses, the results, in the end, are the same: at some point the person can no longer care for him- or herself, and full guardianship must be assumed.

Once we had guardianship and understood Mom's financial situation, we were painfully aware there were no life insurance policies to fall back on. We then took a close look at what monies we had to work with and began to make a plan for what we could do to make sure she was well cared for somewhere.

There was some money in the bank and a few CDs. Our best piece of luck, however, was probably a direct result of the early work of the Alzheimer's on Mom's good judgment.

Because Ray had worked for the U.S. Postal Service, he had a pretty good retirement from the government. Mom had some token income from Leader Dogs, a combination of her "widow's benefits" (Dad had been the public relations director of Leader Dogs for nearly twenty years) and her own retirement benefits from the years following Dad's death, when she worked as a "goodwill ambassador." Ray and Mom had also made some good investments in CDs, and Mom had paid off the mortgage on their home.

No mortgage to pay on the house was our biggest "working" asset. It was, however, a good news/bad news piece of information. The good news: it was owned free and clear. The bad news: the town Mom lived in had buyer-protection laws. In order to sell the house to pay for her care, we would have to take care of a long list of repairs, including some rather costly ones.

For the short term, we decided not to sell the house but to rent it and use the rental income to upgrade the wiring, roofing, bathrooms, and kitchen and to funnel a little money toward paying for Mom's care. The longer we held on to the house, the closer we could get it up to code and ready for sale and have a little extra money to help pay for her care as well. It was a true fountain of wealth in an otherwise sparse financial field.

We held no delusions about the "estate." With very little discussion among the four of us, we unanimously agreed that all the money should be used for Mom's care. More important, we would use the money to buy the best care we could find. If it took all the estate and then some, it just would.

We also decided we should hold on to the house until all other resources were exhausted. We hoped making the repairs would help raise the selling price, giving us more money to spend on her care.

Our bottom line: we could afford to have Mom close to part of the family, safe, and well cared for, as long as she needed to be there. We got lucky because the Chelsea Methodist Home, which was ten minutes from Lolly's, found a place for her in their Alzheimer's wing.

Until you are faced with this decision, you cannot

understand the weight it brings to your shoulders, your hands, and your heart. It is one of the most difficult passages I have ever encountered. It is also tricky and treacherous, because *you* are making a life-changing decision for someone else: someone who may not agree with your decision and, in fact, may adamantly oppose it.

It was not an easy decision. It was not a comfortable decision. But it was a unanimous decision for the four of us.

3

FINDING A HOME

Mom was boss. She was born boss. She lived boss. She was so good at being the boss that if you had met her right before and even right after we gained custody of her, what you would have noticed about her was that she walked and talked like someone in total control. She seemed normal. Which often made it difficult for us to convince other people that there was something wrong with her.

By the time we had gotten help from the Department of Social Services with having Mom tested at the University of Michigan, we had given up on talking with her regular physician. This particular doctor was the same age as Mom and was probably experiencing some aging quirks himself. If we complained to him about Mom's occasional confusion, her memory loss, and her emotional outbursts, he told us these behaviors were normal for someone her age. When we insisted they weren't, he would respond by saying Mom was as healthy as a horse and sharp as a tack.

The diagnosis from the University of Michigan gave us the evidence we needed to gain custody of Mom. At the same time, the doctors and staff at UM were quite clear in their assessment of Mom that despite the fact that she could walk and talk a good game, she was not in any shape to be living on her own. Mom's problems were our problems now, and they weren't going to go away.

By this time, we knew from firsthand experience that we were not fully equipped to take care of Mom in one of our homes. So even before we gained legal custody of her, we began looking for ways to care for her. We had already had the experience of having Ray in a nursing home and knew that that was not a viable option for Mom. So we began looking at retirement centers that had assisted living and Alzheimer's units.

The best facility we found, in terms of its overall program for Alzheimer's victims, was the Chelsea Methodist Home near Lolly. Unfortunately, they didn't have any vacancies in their Alzheimer's wing when we first called them. They did, however, have units available in a new independent living center that they were going to be opening soon.

The social worker we had been working with from Social Services happened to mention to Lolly that the Chelsea Methodist Home was known for providing their residents with a continuum of care. In other words, once they took in a resident, they kept that resident and moved them from level to level of care as their circumstances changed. Which led us to approach the Methodist Home and put down a deposit on one of their independent living units.

The maneuver to get her into the Chelsea Methodist Home was a little tricky because we knew she couldn't be in independent living, plus we didn't have custody of her, so we didn't have the authority to place her anywhere. When we went to tour the facility and talk with the staff, we did not take Mom with us. After seeing the model of the proposed units, we mentioned that we suspected that somewhere down the line, Mom might need to be moved to assisted living. The staff assured us that this would not be a problem. They were sensitive to the changes that sometimes occur in aging and would let us know when they felt it was appropriate for her to move. So we filled out the papers, paid the down payment, and waited.

This may not be one of the more honorable things we have done in our lives, but we were desperate. We did not want to put Mom into a facility that was not designed or committed to taking care of Alzheimer's victims. We knew she needed special attention.

The unit was finished before we had custody, so we began paying rent. During this time, we did not take Mom to meet the staff. She was very volatile and difficult, and we never knew what she would say or do. As fate would have it, though, the director of the home called one afternoon and said she was aware that we hadn't moved Mom into her unit yet, but that she also realized that she had never met Mom. She wanted to know if we could bring her in. Obviously, we were not eager to take Mom in to meet the director. She still had no idea we were making plans to move her—plus, we still didn't have custody. So we stalled.

Finally Lolly had her court date and was granted custody of Mom. About a week later, I flew up to Michigan, and Lolly made an appointment for us at the Methodist Home. Since we now had the legal capacity to move her, it was time to take her to see the home. We hoped that once they met her, they would take her.

We decided to call in the help of our brother, Chuck. Mom liked him best during this time, and we felt that if the idea came from him, she might buy into it. Plus, she was more relaxed around Chuck than she was around the rest of us. With Chuck around, we had the best chance of Mom seeming normal.

We got Mom dressed and told her that Chuck and I were going to go take her to look at apartments. She was agreeable but edgy. She said she liked the apartment she was living in and didn't want to move. When we tried to explain that it wasn't an apartment but Lolly's house, she thought we were crazy. Who's Lolly? she asked. At which point we knew we were doing the right thing. We just hoped the Methodist Home would understand how badly we needed them.

Lolly opted to stay home. The whole thing made her uncomfortable since she was the one who had negotiated the independent living unit. Chuck and I took Mom and hoped for the best.

The director was charming and wonderfully professional. Midway through the tour, she smiled at us and motioned for my brother and me to follow her as she asked another staff member to have a cup of coffee with Mom. My heart skipped a beat. Mom had been unusually confused and just a tad edgy as questions were asked and the various features of the apartment were pointed out. From our point of view, it had not gone well. I didn't know whether to confess or bolt for the parking lot.

We went into the director's office, and she closed the door. Your mother, she said, may not be right for independent living. Had we ever thought about placing her in one of their assisted living units?

At this point, I told her the truth: that we had just recently gotten her evaluated at the University of Michigan and that they believed she had Alzheimer's. The director looked surprised. At first I took the surprise to be one of shock that we had signed a contract for an independent living unit knowing it was not appropriate for Mom. But that was not the case. She was surprised, she said, because she doubted Mom had Alzheimer's. Mom seemed to her, except for some confusion and a little memory loss, to be smart and alert and quite in control.

They had an assisted living unit that was going to be available in the next two weeks, she said, that might be better suited for her. We told her we thought that would be great, and we signed a new contract.

The assisted living unit they had was on a wing where residents took their meals in a main dining room away from their hall. The residents had their own rooms and were free to wander around the facility taking advantage of lectures, classes, and activities. We were apprehensive that Mom could handle the situation but grateful to have her officially placed. We made bets with each other about how long it would take the staff to discover she had Alzheimer's and couldn't be on her own at all.

Lolly bet a week. I bet two. It took ten days before the call came, and in that ten days, it must have been quite something for the staff. Mom refused to eat in the dining room because she said it was too fancy and she couldn't afford it. When the staff tried to explain that the meals were included with her room, she accused them of trying to trick her. She went into other residents' rooms and stole candy and whatever other food she could find. She also wandered away several times and got lost.

In an attempt to help Mom adjust to her new situation, the staff paired her with a "buddy," another resident, to make sure she got from her room to the dining room without trouble. Mom accused the other resident of being in cahoots with the staff. She told the buddy that she knew she was taking her to the dining room so that the staff could go into her room and take what they wanted.

Needless to say, the buddy was quite upset and told the staff what Mom had said to her. They tried to talk to Mom, but she wouldn't listen. She refused to leave her room, and she also refused to eat because she said it was all a plot to get her money, and she wasn't falling for their schemes and lies. When they brought food to her room, she demanded to see the bill. When they couldn't produce a bill, she refused to eat, saying she knew she'd be billed later for everything she ate. She called my sister and me every night asking us to bring her bread and bologna.

Mom's behavior in the Home was not unlike her behavior in Lolly's home. We were all periodically accused of trying to steal her money, of kidnapping her, of holding her prisoner, or of trying to poison her. In a way, it was gratifying to get the call and to know the staff had experienced firsthand what we had been struggling with at home. But in another way, it was really sad. Mom did look normal, and she even sounded normal sometimes, but she wasn't anymore, and there was no denying it.

But just as there was no more denying that Mom had Alzheimer's, she could, on a "good" day, fool someone. Just as she had fooled the director.

Many people, including medical professionals, often ignore or misread the occasional Alzheimer's-like symptom during the first five to seven years of the disease. Which makes the issue of accountability a sticky one.

Alzheimer's is an untested road, both legally and medically. In 1994 an advisory panel on Alzheimer's from the

U.S. Department of Health and Human Services, the Public Health Service, the National Institutes of Health, and the National Institute on Aging made a report to Congress regarding legal issues in both the care and treatment of Alzheimer's disease and related dementias. In their report, they cited, as one of the main difficulties of Alzheimer's, the progressive nature of the disease without clear "stages."

Doctors have difficulty making a clear diagnosis and assessment of the competency of Alzheimer's victims because these victims are unable to accurately assess their own situation and report on what they are experiencing. Like family members, Alzheimer's victims cannot pinpoint when their disease began, which makes establishing a starting point from which to measure decreased competency impossible. As the commission stated: "The expertise and background of the medical witness, oftentimes a family doctor who has treated the patient for years, may not reflect current knowledge of the diagnosis or treatment of Alzheimer's disease."

The same advisory panel that recognized the difficulty of identifying competency for Alzheimer's victims also concluded that "a person in the early stages of Alzheimer's disease retains the legal right to make his or her own decisions absent a court finding of incapacity and may well have the current ability to establish voluntary delegations of decision making."

This conclusion is chilling. Who knows when Mom

was last truly competent and in her "right mind" and able to make decisions? I suspect it was back in 1986, five years before we felt "sure" about our suspicions. And five years before we did anything about them. During the years preceding the "beginning," we now suspect there were "normal" moments and "abnormal" moments in her thought processes. Also, we suspect there were times in the beginning of her decline when she had clear, blinding moments of rational thought.

No one as yet has been able to correctly label the legal or medical moment when someone with dementia moves from making competent decisions to making incompetent ones. And this, unfortunately, makes coming to the decision to take charge or even put someone in assisted living to keep them safe from themselves all the more complicated.

Even after we had placed Mom in assisted living at the Chelsea Methodist Home, then ten days later, on the staff's recommendation, moved her to the Alzheimer's wing, we still had difficulty getting the staff to understand what we had lived through before we came to them.

Shortly after Mom came to live in the Methodist Home, Lolly and I were having a care conference with the staff. They were expressing their concerns about how rapidly she seemed to be declining, given that she had had Alzheimer's for such a short time.

We didn't understand what they were talking about and asked them to explain. They then told us that as far as they were concerned, Mom had had Alzheimer's only since the time she was diagnosed at the University of Michigan. We disagreed with them and said that we were pretty sure Mom had been battling with Alzheimer's for at least six or seven years.

Incredulous, one of the staff members asked us to give them some specific examples of her behavior that might have led us to think she had Alzheimer's. When we began to tell them some of the stories, they agreed with our time line but were still surprised.

"If you've been dealing with this for all these years," the director said, "you must be nearly burned out." We were.

Burnout is just part of the problem. Alzheimer's is sneaky. In the early stages, you have trouble seeing it, then right at the point that you're confident that you can recognize it, Alzheimer's ducks its head again and surprises you.

Two years after Mom moved to the Chelsea Methodist Home, I was visiting her one afternoon and we were taking a walk through the facility together. All around us, people were shuffling about in walkers, bumping against the walls, and talking to themselves. It was a typical day on her floor. Mom, like the other patients, was doing her own version of cruising and mumbling, struggling to get a string of words to stay together. All of a sudden, she grabbed my hand and started to giggle. With her other hand, she made a gentle sweeping arch, as if to say, See what we have here. "You know," she said, pulling me closer in order to whisper in my ear, "sometimes I say to myself, 'Ruth, you really must be crazy to be here.'" Then she giggled again and slipped back into her other world, where words and thoughts get tangled and lost.

It took my breath away.

4

THE LONG STRETCH
OF MIDDLE YEARS

November 1992. We take the twenty-two-hour train ride from Raleigh, North Carolina, to Ann Arbor, Michigan, to have Thanksgiving with Mom, but we cannot tell her we are coming. My brother drives a double shift on his truck route so he can take a three-hour nap, put his son and his wife in his pickup, and drive all night from Paducah, Kentucky, to Michigan to come, too.

We feel lucky this Thanksgiving. We have managed to place Mom in one of the best Alzheimer's units in the area, and she's at last happy. She doesn't, however, know she's being taken care of. She thinks she has a beautiful new house. She believes the people living across the hall from her really live down the street. When she first moved, she thought she worked at the Chelsea Methodist Home. Now she tells us she pitches in only when her neighbors need help or when there's a party or some special event.

If we were to tell her we were coming to see her, she would go immediately to the elevator to wait for us, not knowing day from night, Thanksgiving from New Year's Eve.

Time and space mean nothing to her. Last Christmas we gave her one of those programmable telephones. We installed all our numbers into the memory so all she had to do was push one button to call each of us long distance. We even labeled the buttons. She called me a couple times a day asking me to run errands for her or bring her food. When I tried to explain that I couldn't because I lived in North Carolina, she got angry because I wouldn't do what she wanted. She has since quit calling us because she has forgotten how to use her fancy phone.

We have decided to go to Lolly's house for Thanksgiving this year because over the weekend, we are going to throw a wedding reception for our youngest brother, Chuck. He isn't planning on getting married until next July, but the staff at the Methodist Home have asked us to be a little "creative" about the wedding. July is too far away. Mom is obsessed with his upcoming marriage and is becoming agitated. Also, it is unclear what she will know or remember by next July. We all agree it would be nice for her to believe that he is, at last, married.

Since Lolly has the role of legal guardian and lives in Chelsea, ten minutes from Mom, she sees her the most. It's a lucky break for Mom and the rest of us, but a burden for Lolly. I worry about Lolly more than I do about

Mom. Mom is fine. She's happy, well fed, safe, and feels independent and productive. Lolly, on the other hand, understands what is happening.

Ironically, Alzheimer's victims often cannot recognize their primary caregiver. Such was the case with Mom. When I would call to talk to Mom while she lived with Lolly, she would tell me all about the wonderful people she was staying with, although she couldn't accurately identify them or where she was living. Once we moved her to the Methodist Home, however, she was once again able to remember my sister's name and correctly identify Lolly's children as her grandchildren.

You can laugh about something like that, but it's confusing. It feels bad, and your feelings get hurt, even though your head tells you it's just the disease doing its damage.

If you're the "good kid," the one who calls every Sunday, the one who takes on the responsibility of being the guardian, the one who sends flowers on Mother's Day and tries to do the right thing, Alzheimer's can drive you crazy. The only way to be the happy survivor of an Alzheimer's victim is to lie, and the "good kid" would never lie to her mother.

But that's how we manage to survive and laugh through this time. We lie. It's not an easy thing to do. It feels wrong. It feels like you're living dangerously, because if you get caught, your mother is going to punish you.

Like sins, there are lies of commission and lies of omission. Our first lie for Thanksgiving is not telling Mom we're all coming. Our second is telling her that the reason Chuck and his fiancée aren't eating Thanksgiving dinner with us is that they have flown to Las Vegas to get married. The truth: the only way Chuck could get Friday off from work in order to attend his wedding reception was to work Thanksgiving.

We think the lie about Las Vegas is a great lie. We rehearse it a little and tell the kids. When you're into lying, you've got to make sure all your bases are covered. Once we've got the lie down pat, we've got to decide who is going to deliver it.

Nobody volunteers. Timing is everything when you're telling lies to an Alzheimer's victim. You've got to wait for the lucid moment, the little crack in the window of reality, the few heartbeats where she's with you all the way. Otherwise you've got to repeat yourself, and anyone who's ever told a lie knows repeating the lie is the best way to get caught.

It's my turn. Mom is in Lolly's kitchen. The table is set for turkey and all the fixings. We're standing around trying to take a reading on how the afternoon is going to roll. It's clear Mom doesn't know it's Thanksgiving. She hasn't called anyone by their correct name or any name, which is usually a bad sign. You can see the little kids are making her nervous.

"Where's Chuck?" she asks, clutching her purse in

her hands, looking around the room, trying to get her bearings.

There is this terrible silence. I haven't felt this scared since I was ten. Nobody says anything. Gary, the oldest, looks down at his shoes.

"You're not going to believe this," I tell her, looking at my siblings for support, "but he called this morning. He and Donna are in Las Vegas. They're getting married."

"I just had a feeling," she says, and we all breathe a little easier because we know she got it, "they were going to do that."

"Aren't you glad." The guilt of the lie breaks over me like a wave about to knock me off my feet. "She's a real nice woman. I think Chuck's lucky, don't you?"

"I just had a feeling," she says again.

Gary straightens his glasses and moves into the kitchen to help Lolly carve the turkey.

I trust Lolly's instincts about this fake wedding. She is the one who has the most contact with Mom. She's the one who is going to be left taking care of her after the rest of us pack up and go home. She's also the one who has ordered the cake and talked to the nursing staff and made all the arrangements for the reception to be on the Alzheimer's wing.

Lolly says it's the only way the thing is going to work. It has to be on the Alzheimer's wing because Mom is at her best there. It's where we stand the greatest chance of her remembering. If Lolly says we're having cake and punch and fake wedding pictures on the Alzheimer's wing, then that's what we're doing, and I'm willing to back her one hundred percent.

Chuck doesn't want to do it. He knows it's the "right thing," but he doesn't want to have to spend any time with all those people who have Alzheimer's. It's creepy, and it brings it all too sharply into focus. Chuck wants us to have the cake and the pictures at Lolly's house.

Gary isn't the kind of person to buck the crowd—he never has been. Still, he brings up the question one more time, trying to be sure we should go through with this.

Lolly looks at me, and I tell Gary I think Lolly's right. It has to be at the Alzheimer's wing. He nods his head, and I know he'll be there.

Chuck will, too. We've had to use him for a lot of things in the past couple of years. For the moment, he's the one Mom responds to, so he was the one who drew the short straw to take her to the Methodist Home the first time. Lolly and I set it up, but when the time came for Mom to go, Chuck was the one who convinced her it would be a good place to live. It was Chuck who sold her on the idea of moving.

Chuck has also been the beneficiary. He manages to catch all the credit. Mom believes Chuck bought her a new bed, although Lolly bought it and Tom, her husband, delivered it and set it up. The fancy spread and headboard came with a birthday card signed from the four of us, but Chuck's was the only name she remembered.

Like con artists setting someone up for the sting, we have begun to act like gangsters with Chuck as the mouthpiece.

About six months ago, Lolly, who had just returned from spending an afternoon cleaning Mom's house and painting her garage so we could rent it in order to help pay the bills at the Methodist Home, called me in a fit. Mom had called her and told her she only had one child, Chuck. We both laughed about it and decided that if Chuck was an only child, and if we knew for certain we had siblings, then he couldn't possibly be ours. And if he wasn't ours anymore, then we were no longer responsible for him.

We give Chuck a hard time. We all laugh about the only-child business. It's even funnier since Gary used to claim he wanted to be an only child when he grew up.

We drink a toast to Chuck and his new bride before we carve into the turkey. Mom looks a little bewildered, and we all start talking again about how good Donna is and what a surprise it was they called to say they were going to Las Vegas to get married.

The phone rings. Lolly gets up to answer it, and we all know Chuck is calling to check in to see if the rest of us have arrived. Lolly is great on the phone and manages to chat her way through the conversation as though she's talking to a neighbor, which is what she tells Mom when she hangs up.

There's a lot of food on the table, and it's getting

passed around, and we all sense the confusion Mom feels. It has been more than a year since she could correctly identify a fork from a spoon. Food is complicated. She's not sure what to do with the gravy so she passes it on. She makes a mess of things, putting mashed potatoes on her salad plate, cranberry sauce on her green beans, and generally blowing the conventional wisdom of turkey and stuffing, gravy and sauce.

The older kids giggle but stifle it in a hurry as the rest of us turn on the ice-from-hell look. The kids make Mom nervous. Most of the time they're fairly sensitive to her needs. They know, however, that if they do the same thing she has just done, they will be sent from the table. The situation is funny, yet filled with tension.

Someone makes a joke, and we all laugh. I concentrate on eating the dressing. It's the best yet, and I want to remember the good of the day: we're all here, and Mom's alive and physically well and happy. It's hard, because her disease has taken a toll on us all.

It's a gray day outside. My kids swear they've seen some snow flurries, so we all squint and try to see what they want to see. If we look real hard at one place for a long time, we can see a flake or two.

Mom is tired. She starts asking about how she's going to get home. She wants to know who is going to take her. The boys get elected. For some reason, she does better with the men—maybe she trusts them more, or maybe she doesn't think she can question their judgment. One time when Lolly and I took her back after having her over to the house for a long day last fall, Mom fell apart. She didn't recognize her room, the Alzheimer's wing, her fellow residents, anything. She became frightened and began screaming that she wanted to go home. She said we tricked her. It scared the kids to death. Since then we're more careful about who picks her up and who takes her back, and we try not to have the kids in tow on the return.

She believes she has lost her jacket. We know she left it in her room and try to reassure her it will be there. Next, she's sure we've switched purses on her, which we haven't, and keep showing her the purse and reassuring her it is hers. Her name is written all over it in ballpoint pen. A few months ago, she signed her name on everything she could find. Her purse almost looks as though it has been purposely stamped with the design of her name, like a designer fabric. She studies the writing on her purse as though she doesn't recognize her signature or is unsure of what it says. No one says anything. We've learned not to push, to let her come to some resolution on her own. We do not want to agitate her.

"It's getting dark, and I've got to get going. I left the house empty. There's no one there. I shouldn't be gone for long," she says, then she accepts our hugs and kisses and heads out with Tom, Gary, and Jeff, as though she is being escorted by a bevy of bodyguards.

"Not a good day," Lolly says as she heads back to the kitchen to clean up. "Let's hope tomorrow is better."

We all agree.

* * *

Chuck calls to say he and Donna are running a little behind schedule, and we make plans to meet at the Methodist Home. Gary's running late, too, but manages to pull up just as we're packing the kids into the car. Pat and Jamie, his wife and son, won't be coming because they've decided to spend the day with Pat's sister. Nobody thinks this will present a problem since Mom couldn't make an accurate head count on the best of days anymore.

We swing by the bakery to get the cake. It looks great: pale yellow roses and white bric-a-brac around the edges and a big green frosting "Congratulations Chuck and Donna" emblazoned down the middle of a field of flowers and wedding bells. It's every kid's dream-fix of buttercream frosting.

Donna and Chuck are waiting for us in the lobby when we arrive. My stomach jumps and flops and jitters. *We could get caught*, a little voice screams in my head. She could be having a bad day, and this whole thing could backfire.

Mom is in the television room watching *Star Trek* when we arrive. One of the staff sees the huge cake and realizes there's been a little miscommunication. The reception was supposed to be their dessert today, but somehow the message didn't get quite far enough, and they've just eaten pie with their lunch. The staff member touches my arm and suggests we give them time to "walk it off" a little. My stomach knots up. I'm afraid our plan will fail, but I smile back and say it's no problem because we'll need a little time to set up.

Mom pulls Chuck aside and tells him no one came to get her for Thanksgiving. She tells him she didn't have turkey—in fact, she didn't get anything to eat all day. She tells him we've all abandoned her. Chuck tries to reassure her we did come, she did eat with us, she just forgot. She shakes her head no.

The subject gets changed, and we all start talking about the wedding. Donna shows off her ring. She's dressed in creamy white slacks and a beautiful white sweater with sequins and little seed pearls. She's being an incredible sport. My husband, Jeff, starts taking pictures.

That's the key: pictures. One of the staff comes up and asks what we are going to do if she doesn't remember. We tell her we're taking pictures, lots of pictures. We plan to send them to her as soon as they're developed so she can look at them and the staff can talk about them with her. We decide it will help if there are pictures not only of the family and her friends but also pictures of Mom and the staff with Donna and Chuck.

The nurse nods and goes to tell the rest of the staff. One by one they show up and stand with Mom so we can take pictures with the cake and the smiling bride and groom.

The other residents begin to wander into the room. Donna and Chuck cut the cake. We tell everyone it's a wedding reception for Ruth's youngest son and ask them if they want punch and cake. They want to know who

Ruth is, who her son is, and who we are, so we smile and usher them to tables and cut cake, talk, pour punch, and smile. The kids are having a great time. The residents love having them around. The kids aren't afraid and go from table to table and eat cake, refill punch cups, and talk.

One of the ladies keeps wrapping her cake in her napkin and putting it in her lap, all the while telling the other ladies at her table she hasn't gotten any cake yet. There is a bit of commotion over the "unserved" woman, and we don't know quite what to do, so we cut her another piece.

One thing leads to another, and pretty soon the woman has four or five pieces of cake tightly wrapped in our decorative little wedding napkins all piled in her lap. We switch to serving her punch and let her build up a line of punch cups.

Another woman finishes her cake and folds her napkin. Once it is folded, she tears it into strips, then takes her neighbor's napkin and does the same thing. She works her way around the room, from table to table, folding and tearing napkins until she has a stack of torn napkins nearly two inches thick. No one seems to mind.

We sit and talk with the residents, answering questions over and over again. Many of them have lost their natural affect and seem flat, or smile when they are saying something angry or sad. It is the same with Mom. Words and actions no longer match: interaction is confusing on both sides. In the chaos of the moment, we can see what kind of people all these confused folks once were and can imagine how lively and competent they must have been before the disease took hold. Many of the women on the wing with Mom used to be teachers and nurses. They all, like Mom, have neatly cut and curled hair and wear "good" clothing. You have a sense they led "sensible" lives, kept clean houses, raised children, grew beautiful gardens, had friends, threw parties, had hobbies, volunteered. The loss is overwhelming.

The cake is nearly gone. Everyone has eaten the sugar roses, leaving scraps of cake behind. People begin to wander back to watch television or walk the halls. The staff works hard to bring people by to say hello and have pictures taken standing with Mom.

Mom starts saying it's getting dark. It's her way of telling us we need to go. She doesn't like being out when it's dark, and she doesn't want us to have trouble on the roads. It's not quite three o'clock in the afternoon.

We clean up and prepare to say our good-byes. Mom wants to show us her house. She wants us to see the changes she's made. Her room is the same as it has been since she moved in over a year ago, but we all ooh and aah over the "changes" she shows us. She tells us she only uses this part of the house now and has closed off the rest of it because she doesn't need it anymore. The walls of her room are covered with colored pictures and cut-and-paste artwork she has done in her therapy group. It looks like the work of a young child. She has several bouquets of silk flowers near her window. She tells us she waters them daily. She says she can't believe how long they've lasted.

She can't find her purse and gets confused because our coats are in her closet. The purse is on her desk, and we point out where she has written her name on it again. She takes the purse and holds it as though we might try to take it away from her.

One of the staff members follows us down the hall so she can unlock the elevator. Mom stands back to say her good-byes. She never goes near the elevator. One of the residents occasionally becomes fixated about the elevator. When that happens, the staff puts a library table in front of it. So sometimes you have to move the furniture when you come and go.

When we get back to Lolly's, we all just sit around and talk. Mom liked the reception and all the attention. The cake was beautiful. We are all exhausted.

Lolly tells us two people died on the Alzheimer's wing last week. There's silence. We had all believed that as long as Mom was on the Alzheimer's wing, she was safe. When the disease progressed to the point where it could kill her, we thought she would be moved to a total nursing care unit. We have been living with a false hope that her continued residency on her little happy hall meant she was doing just fine and nothing could harm her.

Chuck says he's read about some new medication, some experimental drug believed to reverse the Alzheimer's process. It is sobering to think about going backward. We have been through so much unraveling and so much grieving, to go backward, to day by day reverse this terrible process, to reexperience all the hurt, confusion, and anger, feels akin to walking through hell again. We are reminded of W. W. Jacobs "The Monkey's Paw," where the family wishes for their son to return from the grave, only to be stalked by his decayed and disfigured body.

We've all read the books. We know about the damage done to our mother's brain. Is there a miracle drug out there that can rebuild the brain? If so, can it do it overnight? Or is the repair as tedious and drawn out as the damage has been?

Gary shakes his head. "It's just too hard to think about," he says, his voice flat, as though he is speaking about the death of a friend. "She was always the boss. I mean, *always* the boss. Now she's like this."

He doesn't need to go on because we know we've crossed over some invisible line that no miracle drug can touch. Mom's gone, and in some quiet and horrible way, we all feel quite alone.

Chuck and Donna have spent the night, and the kids get up early to have their "Christmas" breakfast. It is the Saturday after Thanksgiving, and we've decided that since we are all together, we'll have our family Christmas.

When I get out of the shower, Lolly is in the kitchen scrambling eggs.

"Mom's had two bad days," she says, cracking eggs.

"What would you think about having our Christmas, then going to get her for lunch and after lunch letting her open her presents?"

There are six kids upstairs rattling presents under the tree. It feels like a Christmas morning. There's a lot of excitement and anticipation in the air. It's another lie, a double lie: Christmas when it's not Christmas and a non-Christmas without Mom. But Lolly's right. The chaos and confusion would throw Mom. We stand a chance of making the day work if it is controlled and if all the action and excitement are centered on her.

Last Christmas, the real Christmas, was a disaster. She didn't understand what we were doing with all the packages. She didn't know what presents were hers and kept giving them back and putting other things, stuffed toys and candy and Christmas ornaments, in her bag. She got angry when we took the kids' things away from her and was sullen and agitated during dinner. We are not anxious for a repeat.

"I don't like it," I tell Lolly, and she nods, "but you're right."

Mom's had some good days over the last couple of months, where she's recognized Lolly, made appropriate responses, and generally seemed on top of things. One day she even noticed Lolly had gotten a haircut and commented on how nice it looked. That night Lolly called me to say it was strange, almost as though she was better, that she was herself again.

We open our presents, clean up, and then send Gary

and Tom to go get her. They take his pickup truck. Cole, my youngest, wants to go, too. He loves Gary's big truck. We promise him a ride some other time. It's funny to think of Mom jostling along in the truck sandwiched between Tom and Gary, coming to a Christmas that isn't Christmas that she probably won't remember.

Mom doesn't remember much about yesterday or the wedding. We kid Chuck about being the only child but tread lightly on the reality that Mom doesn't know that the rest of us are her children. When Mom's sister, Jessie, came to visit a few months ago, Mom told her Gary had died a long time ago. Gary is half Navajo. He was adopted when he was an infant. The rest of us are "naturals" and are a fiery blend of Scottish stubbornness and Irish fight. He has the classic American Indian disposition. He is slow to anger. He can't drink worth a damn. He's quiet, and he is our brother to the bone. We cannot joke about Mom thinking he's dead.

No one says anything, but Gary senses she does not know him. He has this great idea about getting a picture of Mom with the four of us while we are together today; then we should all get portraits done of our various families and put the pictures together in a collage so she can see who belongs to whom. Oddly enough, she can correctly identify all of our children as her grandchildren. She can even call Hedy, my daughter, the only granddaughter, by name. She cannot, however, positively identify the rest of us as belonging to her.

She is clearly confused by all the people in Lolly's

house. She doesn't let go of her purse. She keeps showing me the three brass dots decorating the front flap of her purse and tells me she knows the purse is hers because it has those dots. She ignores the fact that her name is written all over the tan vinyl surface. Her fingers trace the dots as though she is reading braille.

One by one the kids come into the family room to sit with her. They watch television together and cuddle. She is responsive to them. Chuck sits with her and talks about the wedding. I mend a hole in the sleeve of her coat and tack down the loose interfacing.

It is her favorite jacket, and she has adorned the lapels with a dozen or more Lions Club pins. Our father was active in Lions Clubs International, and she collected the pins over thirty years of traveling with him. When she talks about Dad, her voice is a little distant and slightly strained as though she is trying to remember him. She tries to give away one of Lolly's favorite childhood dolls to Hedy. Lolly intervenes, saying it was the last doll Dad gave her, and Mom looks a little puzzled. "Yes," she says, looking at the doll and straightening its yellow braids, "Paul was your father."

Dinner is a hodgepodge of leftover Thanksgiving. We eat heartily and laugh a lot. We talk about Donna and Chuck's wedding and the reception at the Methodist Home. Mom seems to be following the conversation and gives her approval or nods when something is said to her. She says she thinks her sister Jessie is coming. We tell her she isn't. She doesn't believe us and keeps saying you can never tell what will happen. She says she just has a feeling Jessie might show up for dinner.

Mom has always had feelings and a strong intuition. It's hard to keep from crying or screaming because although her head is scrambled, her heart is strong. She is strong, as strong and as stubborn as an ox, and would probably live forever if her brain weren't dying.

We clear the dishes and send the kids upstairs to get her Christmas presents. We explain that although it isn't Christmas, Gary and I won't be able to come back up until next summer, so we want to give her our gifts now. "Whatever you want," she says, and shakes her head a little. "I know you can't come."

Donna and Chuck give her a beautiful framed wedding portrait. It is not their wedding picture exactly, but a picture taken of them at a friend's wedding: Donna was a bridesmaid and Chuck is in a tuxedo. It's a great picture and a nice touch. We tell her we'll hang it today when we take her home. She keeps saying how lovely it is and calling Chuck to see it. She tries to give it to him as a gift, and he gives it back. She tries again, and eventually Chuck gets the hint and leaves the room as Donna gives it back to her a fourth time and tells her it is for her, for her house. It is a gift from them to her.

Mom doesn't get it. She puts the picture back in the box and asks Lolly if she wants it. Tom gets a picture hanger and a hammer and lays them near the picture and tells her he'll hang it up in her house when he takes her home. We talk a little about where it might look nice. She's not sure, so we talk a little about her new house and about all the lovely things she has there.

I get a fancy shopping bag with a Christmas scene on it and nice handles and put the hammer and picture in it. We give her more presents.

There are several boxes of candy. Mom has developed a sweet tooth. She likes candy and likes having it around to share with her friends. We've given her lots of little things as well so she'll have lots of packages to open. These include some new cotton socks, a gaudy plastic necklace, which she loves and puts on immediately with the other two necklaces she's wearing, and a small red change purse with a key ring the kids picked out for her.

She likes the change purse, and her face brightens in a way we haven't seen it brighten in a couple of years. The kids show her how it zips and closes and how she can put her keys on the ring. She works the zipper and snaps the snap and asks for her purse so she can get something to put in it. When she opens her purse, it is full of small plastic juice cups from the Methodist Home, and she tries to give one to each of the kids. They are gracious and take them, then give them back, knowing they belong to the Home and she should return them. She gathers them up and stacks them so they'll fit snugly in her bag. She holds the change purse and smiles. It's a great gift.

Three Christmases ago, before we were able to accept or understand what was happening to her, she stood up in the middle of dinner to make an announcement. It was quite uncharacteristic of her, and it was done with such pomp and ceremony that it took us by surprise. She had been edgy all that morning and held on to her purse all day, clicking the tight brass latch open and shut with a nervous kind of tic.

She tapped on the edge of her glass and called for our attention, then took a used envelope out of her purse and began her announcement. I don't remember her hands shaking but thought her voice seemed strange—flat and distant and distressed. She talked for a few minutes without making much sense, our stepfather quiet by her side as though the speech had been rehearsed. Then she called us one by one to stand up. Then she handed out money.

It was a strange gesture, one she had never done before or since. We were all a little uncomfortable but took the crisp bills as directed and took our seats. When the envelope was empty, she sat down and continued with her meal as though nothing had happened.

I carried the money in my purse for almost a year before I spent it, searching for something that reminded me of her. It was the last gift she gave any of us.

We have put all her presents in her pretty bag and have reassured her that Tom will hang the picture as soon as he takes her home today. She says it's late, and she wants to go now. We ask her if she wants to stay for dessert.

Yes, dessert. She likes dessert and says she'll stay. Gary tells her we want to get a picture of her with her kids, and she startles as though he's said something odd.

"I have no kids here," she says, looking around the room, "no kids. I had no kids. No, I had one kid. Only one child. That one there." Then she points to Chuck and walks toward him to hug him. "This is my child," she says, "my only child."

"Oh, Mom," we tease her, "come on, we're your kids, too."

"No," she says, shaking her head, "no, I only had one child. This one, but you," she says, pointing to Lolly, "you look a lot like my family, the Barrs. You could be one of my sister's children."

We try to laugh and all crowd around her, our arms fumbling to link with hers, to draw us all close together. Jeff struggles to get us all in the picture, to get us all in focus.

"Okay, you guys," he calls out, "smile."

5

LOOKING FOR MIRACLES

April 1994. It is ten o'clock on a Wednesday evening. I have just finished conducting a workshop for the winners of the Raleigh Fine Arts Society's high school short story contest. A handful of parents and students have stayed past the workshop to talk and ask for encouragement. When the others at last leave, one lone parent takes me off into a corner and tells me her son is good, really good, but he writes bloody stories, stories she believes we wouldn't accept in this contest.

She wants me to help him. She quickly adds that she does not want me to teach him. She does not believe he needs help with his writing. She thinks his stories are good and that he should continue to write the way he writes. What she wants me to do is help him find a place in this community where his writing will be accepted. She wants me to make some connection in my world for her son.

I give her some suggestions of places he might turn to, people who might be able to help him, but I do not offer to become his mentor. I do not know much about science fiction; nor am I hooked into the science fiction writing/publishing network.

Her desire, however, for her son to find a comfortable and nurturing place for himself strikes a chord with me. As I pull out of the parking lot, too tired to remember clearly if I need to turn left or right to go home, I think about my mother.

Gary drove up from Kentucky to see Mom last weekend. He spent three hours with her one afternoon, and during all that time, she was unable to make a connection with him. She didn't know who he was, who she was, or who they were together. Later, Mom got angry when Lolly, whom Mom didn't recognize either, had to leave. When Lolly was telling Mom it was time for her to leave, an attendant happened by and asked if Mom would like the cup she was carrying to be refilled. My mother, angered and confused and missing the connection between her cup and the man's question, threw the water she had been drinking at him.

My sister sounded tired on the phone when she told the story: tired and drained and aggravated. For the last few years, every family visit and every holiday has been severely touched and even damaged by our mother's illness. It is the first time I have heard Lolly complain or feel resentful, but what she says is the truth: the specter of our mother and her illness has moved across our lives like a shadow we can't shake.

For one clear moment, easing into the string of head-lights going home from the high school workshop, I understand what is happening to our family: we have let go of any chance for a miracle.

Our family has lived by miracles. In 1954, the year Lolly was born, our father was diagnosed with throat cancer. He was not supposed to live. No one with cancer lived back then. But then the first miracle came: radiation treatments.

He was one of the first people in the United States to receive radiation treatments. They were given to him on an experimental basis at the University of Michigan. As experiments go, it wasn't a bad one. Unfortunately, they overestimated how much radiation was needed to cure the disease and managed to damage two-thirds of his lungs in the process, but they made a miracle, and he lived.

Thirteen years and many miracles later, having developed diabetes and undergone surgery for a pacemaker, another life-saving innovation of modern medicine, he died of a massive brain tumor. Still, at no time during his life of illness had we ever let go of the hope of a miracle. We always believed he would get better. We never let ourselves think it was hopeless.

It is hard to hope for miracles with Alzheimer's. Unlike cancer, heart disease, or even AIDS, there are no "good days" where a remission steps in and the patient is given a brief window of normal. There are no miracles. In fact, given the phenomenal destruction to the brain, it is hard to envision what a remission would be like. There is no phase of the disease that you would like to have anyone you know stuck in or returned to because of some medical miracle. There is no remotely satisfactory half-life a miracle might bring.

In fact, the idea of such a "remission" is terrifying. It makes my stomach hurt to think of my mother caught in a moment when her memory is returned and she knows my name, her name, her past, her present, and her grandchildren's names and is confronted by the staggering sadness of all that she has lost.

Over the past few years, as Lolly, Gary, Chuck, and I have talked about some incident, some outburst, some new loss she has experienced, there have been all too many moments when we have stopped and almost simultaneously said: "She isn't really Mom."

Families living with Alzheimer's need more than a big-time medical miracle. We need a way to sort out just how all of us are connected in the world. We need a way to keep ourselves tied together. It is more than flesh and blood. It is history. It is past and promise. It is the shared secrets between people who have known each other for a lifetime.

Although the "warning signs" of Alzheimer's read like a checklist for aging, the disease is more than just an intense version of aging. Yes, when you age, your memory gets fuzzy, little details of events blur together, and you sometimes jumble the past and the present. As you age, or just find yourself pushed by the staggering demands of life, you can sometimes forget where you're going or what you're supposed to be doing. But your mind is not a total blank, and you have emotions.

Alzheimer's takes all that away. The best description of Alzheimer's was given to us by one of the doctors who tested Mom. After describing Mom as a "textbook case," he suggested we tell our children: "When Grandma goes to sleep, the tape recorder in her head, the one recording everything she sees, hears, or thinks, accidentally gets erased, along with a little bit of the past." With Alzheimer's there is no day in the future that will ever be as good as the day you just erased.

And while Alzheimer's is erasing the past, it erases the present, jumbles language, and makes a mess of emotions. It has been a long time since my mother's face showed joy, surprise, recognition, or expectation. It has been a long, long time since any of us have heard her laugh.

And while Alzheimer's is messing with the memory and emotions, it does some interesting things along the way. Earlier in our mother's illness, when she was first moved to the Alzheimer's wing at the Chelsea Methodist Home, the staff took away her cigarettes for safety reasons. They told her they would keep the cigarettes for her in the nurses' office, and she could come down there anytime she wanted to smoke.

Even though the tobacco industry claims nicotine is

not addictive, our mother tried all her life to quit smoking but was never successful. Even when our father was diagnosed with terminal throat and lung cancer, clearly linked to his smoking, she was unable to quit and continued to smoke in the backyard and in secret the rest of her life. In fact, in the years preceding her hospitalization for Alzheimer's, she probably smoked two to two and a half packs a day.

Once the cigarettes were removed from her purse, however, she forgot she smoked and within a day or two quit going to the nurses' station.

She has also forgotten on occasion what her false teeth are for and has discarded her glasses because she forgets they are hers. She is extremely nearsighted and probably can't see two feet in front of her without them.

The cigarettes, teeth, and glasses don't really matter. They are the symptoms. They are visual manifestations of the trouble inside. They are not the things we struggle with when we think about her.

We are like the mother who pulled me aside at the short story contest to whisper her concerns. We want to find a connection. We are looking for something or someone who can "hook our mother up" to this life, our lives, this world again. We watch anxiously for a sign that this person who looks like our mother really *is* our mother. We are looking for a reason to be grabbing for miracles.

Instead, we are gasping for air as we drown along with

her in the dark sea of her never-ending illness. I have quit telling funny stories to our children about what Grandma was like before she became ill because that time is too far gone for me to pull it back again. It is too hard to think about.

We have lost our connection to her memory, to the person within her. We were raised to believe there is a heaven and that when you die, your body, however diseased or damaged in life, is restored whole again as you begin a new life. This new fresh life in heaven enriches and renews everything you did in this life a thousandfold through eternity.

And who will our mother be then? Will she be the mother of our childhood? Will she be the grandmother our children have lost? Or will she be the beautiful and bright high school girl she was so many years before we ever came into her life? Does death depend upon some sweet center of the brain to cast the life eternal? Will she remember everything but the last horrible years when she cursed us and said she had no children, or believed we had abandoned her or died?

6

TRAPPED IN THE MIDDLE YEARS: YOU'RE ALWAYS LOOKING BACK

There are two new women on the Alzheimer's wing. One looks so "normal," I see the kids do a double take because she doesn't wear a staff nametag. I know what they're thinking. They're thinking, *What is she doing here?*

Mom looked like her once. She even fooled the staff when they first met her in 1991. They thought we were wrong about her having Alzheimer's. They thought the doctors who had tested and examined her at the Turner Geriatric Clinic were wrong. Mom talked a good game. She was a great fake.

She was a brilliant woman. The summer after she graduated from high school in 1936, she took the Missouri state teachers' exam and received the highest score on record at that time. She was granted a teaching certificate that August without ever having gone to college and began teaching at a nearby school in Turtle Creek in September.

Mom was not only smart, she was tough. She was the boss, and she ran everything under her jurisdiction or anything that got in her way. She raised four children by herself while our father was "on the road" for Leader Dogs, 300 out of 365 days a year. She cooked, cleaned, checked homework, fixed flat tires, flushed plumbing, gardened, volunteered, did Dad's expense account, balanced the checkbook, and managed music lessons, broken arms, and sibling rivalry without ever missing a beat or breaking down.

She was an amazing woman, and she remained amazing up to the point where the Alzheimer's was so advanced, even she couldn't get around it. We discovered, after we had finally been granted custody of her, that our fears were right: she had been ill a long time. Her financial records for a good six or seven years back were a mess. She had always been a top-notch bookkeeper. She had done all of our father's expense accounts and business records, and she took pride in balancing his expense account and our household budget to the penny.

When we went to the bank to review her accounts, we discovered she had been keeping a minimum of $30,000 in her checking account for the past few years. The bank officer who had always handled Mom's accounts told us she had tried unsuccessfully to get Mom to move her money to a money market fund where it would earn interest. Whenever she tried to talk to Mom about it, Mom would get angry and leave the bank. The bank officer said she thought it was crazy.

It wasn't crazy. It was smart. By keeping $30,000 in her checking account, she could avoid the possibility she might bounce a check. She could eliminate all chance that someone would accidentally discover she had forgotten how to add and subtract.

During this same period, from 1989 to 1991, she managed to rack up a wad of towing and car repair bills. When laid out on a table in chronological order, these bills were a suspicious lot. On a rather regular, sometimes weekly basis, Mom's car was towed because it wouldn't start. The starter was changed a couple of times, as well as the battery. There were also bills for just towing charges and charges for "testing." In one five-month period, she had more than eight hundred dollars in repairs alone.

We believe she must have been having trouble with the sequence of actions it took to start the car: putting it in neutral, inserting the key, turning the key, pressing on the gas until the motor turned over, then putting the car in gear. In other words, she couldn't always remember how to start her car. And the gas station was having a royal flush of a time collecting money for her confusion.

Put in the context of our mother being the sole driver for years, and clocking in hundreds of thousands of miles while taking our father from one speaking engagement to another, this little lapse of memory is staggering. The driver's seat was a second home for her.

The bills from the gas station anger me. The money in the bank, however, makes me sad, because it makes me think that there was a time, a moment early in the disease, when she knew what was happening and was scrambling desperately to deny it, to stop it, in whatever way she could. And the same fierce pride that made her boss made it impossible for her to tell anyone.

Difficulty with seemingly simple tasks that are really a sequence of tasks, like starting a car, is typical of Alzheimer's victims. An unwillingness or even refusal to bathe regularly is a dead giveaway that something is seriously wrong.

In the fall of 1991, when we were coming to grips with our mother's illness while we were trying to gain custody of her, I was in Michigan to help my sister. It was a very difficult time, and we were utterly exhausted with all the paperwork, the prognosis, and the staggering reality of what we were going to have to do to help her live comfortably.

Mom was living with Lolly at the time. I had just arrived, and Lolly was clearly at her wit's end. She said she had been trying to talk Mom into taking a bath for the past week and had failed. She asked if I could bathe her and change her clothes so that we could take her to the Turner Clinic for some testing.

I got towels and some fresh clothes and took Mom into the bathroom. She was in a belligerent mood, which was typical of her during this time. When I urged her to come on and get into the shower, she got angry.

Mom was still big and strong and not one to tangle with either verbally or physically. Not wanting a fight, I just backed off a little and asked her to please take a shower so we could get dressed and go.

Luckily, her anger broke for a moment, and I saw she was afraid. I waited until she could compose herself, then offered to help her take off her clothes.

She was amused. I helped her with her blouse and slacks, then had her sit down to take off her shoes and socks. Then she looked at me and said, pointing to her underwear and bra, "These, too? I have to take off these?"

When I said yes, she asked why. When I told her they would get wet if she wore them into the shower, she was surprised but agreed to take them off.

She didn't know what the soap was or what she was to do with it. She seemed afraid of the washcloth and didn't know what it was called or how it should be used. When I washed her hair, she became unhinged.

It was as though it was the first time she had ever bathed. It was all new and strange and confusing. When I wrapped her in a towel and got her out of the shower, she was close to tears. "It's very hard," she said. I understood: there were so many steps, so many tiny tasks making up bathing, it was hard to remember them all and to remember how and when to do them.

My mother has never acknowledged there is anything wrong with her. She has never talked about having Alzheimer's. In fact, during a visit with her in August 1994, the staff at the Methodist Home said it was rather unnerving to them when Mom talked about her sister Geneva who has Alzheimer's. When she talks about Geneva, she cries, saying how terrible it is that Geneva cannot remember anything, and how sad it is when someone has lost her past.

One day during this same visit, we were sitting on a balcony in the sunshine with the children, and she began crying uncontrollably. Then just as suddenly, she stopped. When she stopped crying, she seemed surprised to look up and see the children were with us. She asked what their names were, and Lolly and I told her. She kept asking over and over, and we kept telling her, reminding her they were her grandchildren and that three of them had family names from her family as their middle names.

It was clear that this was confusing to her, so I asked her if she had a middle name. She thought about it for a minute and nodded her head yes. I asked her what her middle name was, and she hesitated for a minute before she spoke. "Laura," she said. "My middle name is Laura."

Lolly's real name is Laura. Mom's middle name is Margaret.

Although the doctors who examined her at the Turner

Geriatric Clinic in 1991 described Mom as a "textbook" case, everyone reacts to Alzheimer's differently. Some get depressed and withdrawn, some angry and belligerent, some confused and weepy, and some just shut down. Also, there's no constant. Someone might be angry at first, then become weepy. Some are violent. Many of the people who have lived with Mom on Wesley Hall seem caved in. They wander. They sit. They mumble. They walk up and down the halls talking to themselves. They become obsessed with possessions, and the biggest hassle seems to be what chairs "belong" to which people.

In the summer of 1994, Mom had taken possession of a large wooden rocking chair near the elevator. Earlier it was a different chair. One day a man made the mistake of sitting in "her" chair. When she saw him sit down, she flew down the hall and pushed him out of it.

We have witnessed any number of tussles regarding newspapers, shawls, books, chairs, and pocketbooks. The pocketbooks seem to be another "symptom" of the disease.

Mom carried one everywhere for the first couple of years. She had several of them, and the minute she let go of one purse, she was sure it was lost and would panic. Which meant we either found that one or went and got another for her to carry to calm her.

The first year she lived at the Chelsea Methodist Home, we gave Mom twenty dollars in one-dollar bills so she would have money in her purse. The staff didn't like it because she was always giving the money away to the other residents if they said they needed it. Many of the people we've met on Wesley Hall talk about money. More specifically, they talk about not having enough money. It is a source of worry and obsession.

We thought twenty dollars every couple of months or so was a cheap price to pay for Mom's peace of mind. A wad of one-dollar bills stuffed in her purse seemed to give her reassurance that she had a lot of money. It also gave her a sense that she could do something for someone else. She rather enjoyed giving her money away one dollar at a time, and we thought it was fine for her to do something that gave her pleasure.

Despite her toughness, she has always been very nurturing. Despite the ravages of her disease, she continues to be nurturing. The problems the staff have with her center on her concern for other patients and her desire to help them. Having people around her in distress, unfortunately, distresses her.

We have been very lucky Mom has been so nurturing, outgoing, and feisty during her decline. It's clear she isn't easy for the staff to handle. She's not easy for us to handle. But she's interesting, and even when she can't make sense, her presence commands a certain amount of attention and respect, and the staff respond to her.

Whenever we leave Wesley Hall for a walk around the grounds, everyone speaks to Mom. They all call her by her name, and she always calls back with some little babble or banter. Sometimes her responses make sense. Most often they don't.

The two new women—the ones who look normal—carry purses. They don't have them in hand, by the handles, but carry them in their arms close to their chests. They look worried and follow us around asking questions. They want to touch the children. The children are patient and stand still. They talk to the women. The women smile. They start to talk. What they say doesn't make sense. It never does. The children are used to it, but I see Hedy is uncomfortable. I look at what she is looking at, and I see that the shorter woman, the one who is a little plump and carries a white purse, has written her name on her purse over and over again in ballpoint pen, the same way Mom did a few years ago. I know what Hedy is thinking. I know she wonders if Mom can remember when she carried a purse. She also wonders how long this woman will carry her purse before she forgets it is hers. She wonders, as I do, when it will all end.

7

AUGUST 1994

Sarah, one of the women who has been on the Alzheimer's unit, Wesley Hall, for the last three years with Mom, is having a bad day. For the last couple of days we've visited, she's been in the halls searching for something. It has left her agitated and fragile.

Mom senses Sarah's agitation, and although she's in a relatively good frame of mind, she keeps watching her. We all watch Sarah because we are afraid she's going to blow.

The day before, Sarah tried to pull an electrical box off the wall with her hands. She said *it* was hidden there. The attendant tried to soothe her as she deftly moved Sarah away from the box while another attendant pushed a tall-upholstered chair in front of the box to keep it hidden from sight. Instead of solving the problem, hiding the box only heightened Sarah's search for *it*.

Sarah's nervousness and obsessive searching make Mom jittery, so we take a walk down the hall. Sarah follows us, talking to herself, calling out to us as we cruise down to the end of the hall, where the big picture window looks out onto a field.

Mom likes to look out the window and show me the trees and tell me something about what's out there and about how the leaves sometimes "get" brown. Her sentences and ideas lately have jumbled like bits of broken glass and rarely follow a clean sequence, but they manage in their context to make an idea or thought. I know that, when she talks about the trees being green sometimes and brown other times, she knows fall is coming, although the words *autumn, fall, winter, spring,* and *summer* have long since left her brain.

Mom is just beginning to show me the trees when I hear Sarah behind us. I assume she's going to join us, so I turn to say something to her. Just as I do, she turns away from me and runs to the fire escape door.

I'm frozen. I'm trapped between Mom and Sarah. I can't let go of Mom, who now uses my hand or my outstretched arm for balance, and I can't summon the nerve to grab Sarah and stop her. I don't know what Sarah would do. I have no idea if she would turn and hit me. She, like Mom, is unpredictable.

While I watch, Sarah hits the crash bar hard with both hands. The alarm screams out. Mom lets go of my arm and covers her ears. We are standing so close to the alarm, the ringing is terrifying, as though the sound weren't coming from some small box but from within us, warning us something bad is going to happen.

I see an attendant come running down the hall, fumbling with her keys. I look for Sarah. She is standing there, her hands still on the bar, a smile spreading across her face. She is enjoying the ringing of the alarm the way I might enjoy a symphony.

Mom starts to cry. The attendant puts one arm around Sarah, steps between Sarah and the door, and reaches up to the alarm with her other hand to shut it off with a key.

I don't know what to do besides tell the attendant I'm sorry, I couldn't stop her. She assures me it's fine, because the patients never go through the door. The sound of the alarm stops them.

I can see her looking down the hall at the other resident she left in order to stop the alarm. I tell her I'll take Sarah for her. Mom and I will walk a little with her. The attendant thanks me and heads back down the hall.

Sarah is still searching for *it*. I take Mom's hand and tell her everything is fine. As the three of us head down the hall, Sarah kisses her fingertips and touches the fire door affectionately. She seems calmer, which serves to reassure Mom that all is fine again.

As we amble down the hall, I tell Sarah I'll help her look in her room for *it*. I'm sure, I try to reassure her, *it* is in her room.

I have never been in Sarah's room. There's no reason for me to have ever been there, and I am unprepared for what I see.

As I turn the knob and swing the door open, I am confronted with a room filled with oil paintings: beautiful, powerful oil paintings. And I know, even before I summon the nerve to look at the bold signature scrawled across the bottom, that they are Sarah's.

There are landscapes, a still life or two, all of them far more than competent. They are exquisite. They are the work of a gifted artist.

The painting that stays with me, the one I see when I close my eyes now, is one of the largest ones, hung on the wall opposite her door. It is a picture of a dark-skinned man, perhaps a Mexican, with a bandanna tied across his forehead. He is leaning back. His face is serene, and in his hands he holds the reins of two white horses, their faces distorted with strain trying to push forward as he calmly holds them back.

Sarah pushes me aside to look into her room. *It* isn't there, she tells me, then moves on down the hall, still searching.

An attendant comes toward me. I am still standing in Sarah's doorway. My mother is holding my hand.

"They're hers, aren't they," I say to the attendant.

She nods yes, then turns her head away, as though she too cannot face the loss of the life of this artist.

We both know she is gone. The woman, strong, brilliant, talented, who painted these pictures, is dead.

Sarah's pictures are a tangible expression of the grief we feel when we visit Mom. Sarah's pictures are like the AIDS quilt that now covers nearly a mile of loss, fifteen feet wide. If you crawled under it, its weight could smother you.

When I think about Sarah's pictures, I think about the empty words of my doctor trying to reassure me I will not be a victim of Alzheimer's. "People who have active mental lives, people who continue to work and are creative," she says, citing the studies, "are less likely to have Alzheimer's than those who do not." The argument sounds reasonable. It sounds like it might have some medical basis, some credible rationale. It sounds like something I can comfortably cling to.

It isn't true. Sarah's pictures prove it. And the loss you feel when you look at the pictures and see Sarah wandering the halls looking for *it* is so deep, so wide, it could swallow you whole.

I take my mother's hand and walk her down the hall. I do not want her to see these pictures. I do not want her to know that the woman who just crashed through the fire escape door was once an artist. I do not want her to know she herself was once a brilliant woman who ran a household and worked in her community and was respected by everyone who knew her. I do not want her to know what is happening to her. I want to sit by her, hold her hand, tell her everything is going to be fine, and hope she believes me.

8

SORTING THROUGH THE MEDICAL MODEL

Medicine is a science. And, like all good sciences, it works hard to develop a means of codifying and classifying as it makes new discoveries. These codes and classifications create clear guidelines to help physicians make correct diagnoses.

With most diseases, the physician sees a patient during the early stages and is knowledgeable of those stages and how they progress. These early signs help the physician make an early diagnosis and take proper medical precautions. Sometimes diagnosis in an early stage can forestall or even stop the spread of a disease and improve the chances of recovery and survival.

In this early diagnosis and prevention model, Alzheimer's presents some unique problems. First, patients and patients' families rarely seek medical help during the "early onset" stages. Second, even if they did, there is not, to date, anything the physician can do to stop or even slow down the debilitating dementia parade.

In August 1994, after Mom had been a resident of the Alzheimer's wing for three years, Lolly and I met with the head nurse and resident director to talk. Mom had been extremely depressed that summer. She cried all the time and was agitated. They had tried various medications on her with little success. We asked to meet with them because we were worried they might at some time, out of exasperation, resort to restraining her in order to control her. We did not want them to restrain her. We believed she was claustrophobic and any attempt to restrain her would serve only to make her lash out in anger. The thought of them having to restrain her made my stomach knot and twist.

The staff sensed our discomfort. The director of nursing looked at the chart spread out on her lap then up at us. She said they were having as hard a time with Mom's decline as we were because it all seemed so rapid, so sudden, especially since she had only had Alzheimer's for three years.

Her remark was like a whiplash. I couldn't believe I was hearing this again. Three years! I felt a scream strangling in my throat. I felt betrayed. Hadn't we told them before? Didn't they know what was going on? I could see my sister move to the edge of her seat before she spoke. I knew her voice was going to be high and loud and strained. It had not been three years. It had been more like ten. But both Lolly and I knew before we started to talk that, as far as they were concerned, it had been three years.

Many medical professionals have a different take on this disease from those who live it. For them, the disease begins when the patient and/or the family come to them for help. The office visit in which the physician confirms the family's suspicions signals the starting point. In their defense, there's no way for them to know any better because they have not lived through the circumstances that brought the family to see them.

For the families, it is different. There are months and oftentimes years of fuzzy moments. Unfortunately, it is easiest to identify the early onset years once you've passed them. Hindsight, however, is not helpful. What do those early onset years look like? What types of behavior signal that something is going wrong?

As outlined by the Alzheimer's Association, the ten warning signs of Alzheimer's are:

1. Recent memory loss that affects job skills. (They note that it is normal to occasionally forget names, phone numbers, assignments, or appointments, but that dementia, such as Alzheimer's, causes people to forget things more often and not remember them later. Alzheimer's victims might also ask the same question repeatedly, not remembering the answer or realizing they have asked the question before.)
2. Difficulty performing familiar tasks.
3. Problems with language, i.e., forgetting simple

words or substituting inappropriate words, thereby making a sentence incomprehensible.

4. Disorientation of time and place. For example, getting lost in a familiar shopping mall or while taking a walk in the neighborhood or other familiar place.

5. Poor or decreased judgment.

6. Problems with abstract thinking.

7. Misplacing things. (They duly note that a person with Alzheimer's disease may do more than misplace something. They might put things in inappropriate places such as putting an iron in the freezer or a wristwatch in the sugar bowl.)

8. Changes in mood or behavior: rapid, unexplained mood swings from calm to tears, anger to calm, and back again in a few moments.

9. Changes in personality.

10. Loss of initiative.

This ten-warning-signs model comes from the American Cancer Society's "Ten Warning Signs of Cancer" public awareness program. But changes in mood, behavior, and personality are considerably harder to monitor than the growth of a mole. Many of the Alzheimer's symptoms can be easily overlooked or, worse, misdiagnosed as symptoms of depression.

The American Psychiatric Association (APA), in its

publication on Alzheimer's, gives a list of symptoms of depression that are capable of mimicking or complicating Alzheimer's disease, which includes:

- Unexplained weakness or fatigue, dizzy spells, low energy
- Stomachaches, indigestion, constipation; urinary disturbances
- Change in eating habits, appetite, and weight
- Sleep disturbances
- Slowed or more agitated movement
- Feelings of tension, anxiety, or irritability
- Loss of initiative; inability to enjoy activities once enjoyed
- Indecisiveness, apathy, boredom, indifference
- Poor attention and concentration
- Tendency to cry and become upset over minor issues and events; low self-esteem; feelings of worthlessness, hopelessness, helplessness, inappropriate guilt
- Thoughts of suicide

The APA checklist of Alzheimer's disease symptoms includes:

- Loss of short-term memory occurs: person can't learn new information.
- Loss of long-term memory occurs: person can't remember personal information, such as birthplace or occupation.
- Judgment is impaired.

- Aphasia develops: patient can't recall words or understand the meaning of common words.
- Apraxia develops: patient loses control over muscles and can't, for example, button shirts or operate zippers.
- Patient loses spatial abilities and can't assemble blocks, arrange sticks in a certain order, or copy a three-dimensional figure
- Personality changes: patient may become unusually angry, irritable, quiet, confused.

The American Psychiatric Association ends its list with a disclaimer: "Presence of any or all of these symptoms is not a sure indicator of Alzheimer's disease; only a complete examination by a psychiatrist or other physician can confirm the diagnosis."

Both associations provide helpful insights into the early stages, but Alzheimer's defies easy diagnosis. In fact, despite numerous new medical and cognitive diagnostic tests, the only definitive "test" for Alzheimer's is still an autopsy.

In light of the aging "process," many of the warning signs seem part of the normal baggage of growing old: forgetfulness; an occasional fumbling with a button or zipper; changes in eating and sleeping habits; misplacing car keys, a purse, the grocery list. And it is natural for family members to see some of these behaviors as just affectations of aging instead of blinking red lights of trouble.

Even if you suspect something is wrong and you can clearly identify that your family member has exhibited one or more of the characteristic behaviors of Alzheimer's, what do you do? Imagine how difficult it would be to convince a parent or a spouse that they need to go to a doctor because you suspect their recent oversight of your birthday/anniversary or their memory lapse over how to light the pilot light on their stove means they have dementia.

I have yet to meet anyone who claims to have made an "early diagnosis" of Alzheimer's in a family member. Instead, I know dozens of people who sadly admit they can piece together the decline once they "look back" over what may be years of irrational behavior. If you're living it, the best insight, unfortunately, is hindsight.

In retrospect, we should have known something was wrong when our mother didn't want to bring out her Christmas tree in 1989. Mom loved Christmas. She especially loved her tree. And she was a bit eccentric about it.

Years ago she bought an expensive artificial tree and spent hours carefully decorating it with all the ornaments we had made in school, as well as the ones she had bought and collected, tying them on with red velvet ribbons. She thought the tree was so beautiful, she never took it down but kept it instead, all year round, covered with a sheet in the corner of the basement, which was more a family room than a basement. It was the place where Mom and Ray entertained.

When you're starting with someone who's eccentric, it's hard to tell when they cross the line. My mother's penchant for doing what she felt like and saying what she thought made it just that much more difficult for us to be sure her erratic behavior was out of her range of normal.

But in 1989 she just didn't want to bother getting the tree out of the corner, or putting any decorations around the house. She also told me I was stupid for wanting to because it was too much work, too much fuss, too much silliness. This wasn't like her at all, but there was so much that wasn't like her during that time, it was hard to sort out what was happening.

We let the incident pass. We decided she was just being crotchety. Her behavior wasn't life threatening, certainly nothing to give us cause to drag her to the doctor. In retrospect, it was one of those early signs we missed. Or it was one we chose to ignore.

If I knew then what I know now—that not bringing out the Christmas tree probably meant she also didn't know how to light her stove if the pilot light went out, or take a bath—I would have done something. But I didn't know, and even armed with the sharpest of hindsight, I do not have a better list than either the Alzheimer's Association's or the American Psychiatric Association's for determining if someone you love is in trouble. I do not have any answers or hard-core truths.

The "onset" of Alzheimer's is a tricky one. If you suspect something is wrong, you should see a physician immediately. Make a list of the "strange" activities and uncharacteristic episodes that concern you. Give the doctors as much information as possible. They will have no magic medicine to change what is happening, but they will be able to eliminate other possible causes. And they can alert you to other things to watch for. Even though you cannot stop Alzheimer's, understanding what is happening can help you take better care of the person you love.

It is, however, as I also know, difficult to convince someone they ought to see a doctor because their memory is playing tricks on them. It's also sometimes difficult to convince a doctor that this experience of memory loss is more than the normal aging process.

So when we had a chance to speak with the director of the Alzheimer's wing, and she voiced her surprise at Mom's rapid decline, we told our story once again. We hoped she and the staff would make notes and understand that Mom had not had Alzheimer's for three years but for ten.

More than likely all the families with patients on her ward have experiences similar to ours. Victims of Alzheimer's, including the patients as well as their families, need to begin talking to the medical professionals. We need to tell our stories so the knowledge base increases and we are all more aware of what is happening, when it is happening—not afterward, when it is too late to do anything to help.

9

MOTHERS AND DAUGHTERS AND GRANDMOTHERS

I have dreams sometimes where Mom is sick, but she's sick in a wheelchair, or maybe has cancer, or her arm is bandaged, but her face is full and animated. In these dreams, we laugh together and talk.

We have long conversations, sit close to each other, and hold hands. We talk about taking a trip together. She tells me, as she used to tell me when I was a child, how she would like to see the windmills in Holland. I tell her I'll take her, and we begin to make plans.

When I wake from these dreams, my stomach hurts. I will never take my mother to see the windmills. Not only that, but I am afraid to take her out of the Methodist Home. I am afraid she might hit someone or grab the steering wheel of the car while I am driving. I am afraid she might panic, get angry, lash out, and cry uncontrollably because it's getting dark and she wants to go home. I am afraid she won't recognize the building where she lives when I bring her back and she'll be upset when I try to leave her there.

She used to know my daughter's name. Hedy is her only granddaughter, and Mom would once beam with recognition when she saw her. When she couldn't recognize me as her daughter, she could still name Hedy.

In return, Hedy loves her unconditionally. Ironically, the last time my mother came to visit us was in 1984, when I was pregnant with Hedy.

By then she had three grandsons. She had always wanted a granddaughter and kept telling me when I was pregnant, it had to be a girl for her. I had a rough pregnancy. I was exhausted and sick. I had a blood clot in one leg and spent the majority of the pregnancy in bed. Before Mom's visit, I had made the mistake of telling her I honestly didn't care whether it was a boy or a girl, I just wanted the baby to come.

Since I was unable to travel because of the complications with the pregnancy, my mother and Ray came to North Carolina to visit us. They were doing some extensive remodeling of the Raleigh airport during this time, and because of this, I couldn't meet them at the gate. Instead, I had to stand at the end of a long construction ramp to pick them up. As soon as Mom stepped off the plane and onto the ramp, she started yelling at me. You could hear her all over the airport.

"If it's not a girl," she screamed, "it's because you haven't wished it to be a girl. I know you. You're doing this to hurt me. You haven't wished, have you? You just want to hurt me. You just want to make sure I don't ever have a granddaughter. That's just like you."

I was very pregnant, and it was obvious I was the focus of her tirade. People started to laugh. When she heard them laugh, she got madder. By the time she got to the end of the ramp and I tried to hug her hello, she was steaming. She pushed me aside and told me not to bother.

She stayed mad at me during the entire visit. In fact, she remained mad at me for the next couple of years. It was an unexplained anger with no particular focus. My brothers and sister kept saying I must have done something to make her angry. I didn't understand what was happening, and I couldn't imagine, for the life of me, what I had done.

Her actions at the airport and during her visit were not only irrational, they were unlike her. She had always been opinionated and sometimes critical, but never mean-spirited. In fact, despite her gruffness, she was always loving. I began to worry something might be wrong with her. Unfortunately, it would be many years and many harsh and hurtful words later before we understood just what was happening to her and to us.

Despite my mother's belief that I was not wishing hard enough, I did have a girl, and Mom loved her. And Hedy, despite the fact that she never knew her grandmother when she was well, loved her back.

But when we came to visit her in the fall of 1994, Mom no longer knew Hedy's name or that she was her granddaughter. It was painful to watch. I didn't know what to do. I needed to be there for my mother, even though she didn't know who I was, and I also had to protect my daughter.

Caught in the crossfire, I stood by and watched as my mother sputtered and cried and mumbled and jumbled her way through a myriad of thoughts and confusion. My nine-year-old daughter was visibly heartbroken that her grandmother didn't know her. When Hedy moved closer to hug her, Mom screamed at her. After she screamed, Hedy moved farther and farther away from Mom until she was, during one scary, volatile moment, standing in a corner of my mother's room with her hands covering her face as if to protect herself from what she heard and saw.

I worry about my children's memories of their grandmother. Mom, since the Alzheimer's, is sometimes sweet, childlike, and calm. She is also erratic, angry, irrational, and crazy in her speech and actions. Much of the time she is so tense and wound up, she feels dangerous.

I was much older than Hedy when my grandmother, my mother's mother, started showing signs of dementia. Unlike Hedy, I was one of many granddaughters. My grandmother had fourteen children, and all fourteen children bore children. By the time I was ten or eleven, I was one of a throng of grandchildren.

The memories of my grandmother that I struggle to hold on to smell like baking powder biscuits and buttermilk. We visited her each summer at her home in Big Creek, and when we arrived, Grandmother would come out onto the sagging wooden porch of her tiny house and dry her hands on her apron before adjusting her delicate gold-framed glasses.

"Let me see," she'd say, her voice quivering, lips working a little nervously. "Come here," she'd call, holding out her arms so I could bury myself in the flour-dusted folds of her apron. "You're the tallest one. You must be Carrie Jane, Ruth's daughter. Yes, Carrie Jane."

When Grandfather died in the fall of 1966, Grandma "lost her mind." When Grandma became ill, my mother's thirteen brothers and sisters and their spouses, who were scattered all over the United States, pooled their resources to help care for her.

Grandma lived in Big Creek in the Ozarks, near Bunker, Missouri. She and Grandpa settled there ten years after they got married. Other than the little traveling they did, following Grandpa's jobs with the railroad the first ten years of their marriage, Grandma had never been anywhere on a bus, train, or plane. In fact, except for an occasional ride to church or town in Grandpa's car, I don't think she ever left the Bunker area again until Grandpa died.

When Grandpa died, Grandma's world fell apart. She started crying all the time, saying she wanted to go see John in Connecticut, or Polly in Minnesota, or my mother, Ruth, in Michigan. On Mom's urging, the family put Grandma on a plane and sent her to stay with us.

It was the one and only time Grandma ever flew. I was fifteen years old when she came to visit. My mother went to the airport to pick her up. She was very excited at the prospect of having her mother stay with us. It was the only time her mother had ever visited her home, and she was anxious to show it off to her.

Unfortunately, by the time they got from the airport to our house, Grandma had already begun insisting she wanted to go somewhere else. Mom was struggling to remain calm when she unpacked Grandma's bags, but she became unraveled when Grandma started insisting she didn't know my mother. When Mom said she was her daughter, Grandma looked at her incredulously and said quite clearly that she had no living children. They were all dead.

At this pronouncement, Mom began to get edgy. She kept telling Grandma over and over again that she was her daughter. As further proof of this fact, she would patiently go down the list of children, all living, and tell their names and their spouses' names and all their living children's names.

Grandma just stared at her. Later, she told Mom they had gone to high school together. When Mom corrected her, saying she was her daughter, not someone she grew up with, Grandma got angry and nervous.

It was a terrifying time. Grandma was like a frightened

animal. Whenever my father would walk into the room, she would scream, grab my arm, and ask who he was, or who my mother was, or beg me to take her to Polly's house. Time and space meant nothing to her. She was afraid to eat. She told me once she thought "they" were trying to poison her. She wandered the house at night coming into our rooms and waking us, crying and begging us to take her home.

In less than a week's time, Grandma was on a plane back to Missouri. This was the last time I saw my grandmother, and whenever the memories of her, frightened, confused, and lost, crowd into my mind, I try to force them out. I bury my face again in the memory of her big dusty apron. I want more than anything to believe my grandmother loved me, although she did not always know my name.

She died a couple of years later in the Madison Memorial Hospital. The ghost of her fear and confusion filled our house and our lives for a long time after.

I do not believe we should raise children to expect "happily ever after" throughout their lives. Witnessing this kind of mental unraveling, however, is the grand stuff of nightmares, which leaves you wondering what to tell your children.

When one of Mom's doctors suggested we tell our children that Grandma's brain was like a malfunctioning tape recorder erasing what you say, then erasing a couple of days in the past each time she sleeps, I thought it an easy image and concept to grasp. It is an acceptable way to think about Grandma's crazy statements, her nervousness, her inability to remember we visited her yesterday, or just ate dinner, or that I am her daughter and they are her grandchildren.

As she deteriorates, unfortunately, the children's questions get more complicated and harder to explain. They want to know how Grandma is going to die. They want to know what it will be like when they visit her the next time. They want to know if we can still take her out for an ice cream or to Lolly's house for Christmas morning.

They are jumpy when the phone rings at odd times. My daughter wants to know if I'll get Alzheimer's, and if I do, what should she do. My youngest son makes me promise I won't get sick, ever. They want to know if Alzheimer's is contagious, if they can get it.

I tell them no, I hope I won't get Alzheimer's. I promise them I'll take good care of myself, but I tell them I can't promise I won't ever get sick. And I tell them over and over again that Alzheimer's is not contagious and that it is fine for them to hug their grandmother.

Since Grandma clearly had some form of dementia and Mom and two of her sisters are victims of Alzheimer's, there is that worry that we might be in line for trouble. But the threat of Alzheimer's in the future seems less important than quieting my children's fears today.

10

FROM MODERATE TO SEVERE ALZHEIMER'S

I saw Mom four weeks ago. Lolly has called me or I have called her at least twice a week since then to keep up with what's happening.

Mom has started falling. When Lolly went to visit her, a couple of days after I left, she noticed Mom's right foot would flop in an odd fashion whenever she sat down and crossed her legs. Lolly thinks Mom also seemed extremely pigeon-toed and awkward in her gait. She thinks this might be the cause of Mom's falls.

The staff asked Lolly to take Mom for an orthopedic evaluation. She made the appointment, but by the time the appointment came, Mom had fallen several more times, and the staff was trying to get her to use a walker.

Mom angrily rejected the walker. So they tried a wheelchair. The wheelchair didn't make her mad, but she wouldn't stay in it, and whenever she got out of it, she fell again. In order to encourage her to stay in the wheelchair, the staff added a "soft" restraint meant to remind Mom to stay seated in her chair. The restraint agitated her.

We have always known Mom is claustrophobic. She is one of those people who can't stand tight clothes or tight places. She nearly ripped the seat belts out of the car when the car manufacturers first introduced them.

We have all dreaded the day when she would either become immobile or immobilized. Everyone has his or her own version of Orwell's "Room 101." Being constrained, immobile, without will or "wheels" was Mom's. To see this personal hell coming, to know it's going to happen, and to realize you are going to have to watch it happen, is staggering.

Lolly called to tell me the staff had obtained permission from her attending physician to restrain Mom. Her behavior had become so erratic, the staff felt they could no longer control her. They also couldn't keep her in her chair. They were afraid she would fall and break a hip, shoulder, or arm or even take someone else down with her. This new twist in her battle with Alzheimer's was one we had known was inevitable, but nonetheless I had trouble accepting it.

A few days after the restraining order, when Lolly put Mom in the car to go to see an orthopedist and tried to buckle her seat belt for her, Mom freaked. She thought Lolly was trying to restrain her or tie her into the car, and she fought against her. "Buckling up" was quite a battle. Lolly was rattled and exhausted before she ever left the parking lot.

The orthopedist did not have particularly good news. Scarring from a surgically fused ruptured disk, done thirty years earlier, was probably the source of the problem with her foot. Since Mom was unable to answer any questions during the examination, the doctor guessed the nerve that allowed Mom to flex her foot and point her toe had given out. Who knew if it was in any way connected with neurological damage from the Alzheimer's? It was, however, made far more complicated by the Alzheimer's.

The solution to the problem seemed simple enough: Mom was to wear a leg brace. If the brace didn't make mobility possible, she would then have to use a walker or a wheelchair. Easier said than done.

Lolly talked to Mom about the problem. She tried to explain that her foot had quit working, and if she kept trying to walk, she would fall. Lolly was calm and repeated the information over and over, stressing how important it was for Mom not to try to walk, because if she tried to walk unaided, she would fall.

The more Lolly talked to Mom about the importance of not trying to walk, the more agitated Mom became. Eventually she responded by declaring she was strong. And she was: strong as an ox and stubborn as a knot in a pine tree.

When Lolly brought Mom back to the Methodist Home after her visit to the orthopedist, the staff informed Lolly that they were not sure they could continue to keep Mom on the Alzheimer's wing. The falling incidents, her heightened agitation, her irrational behavior, punctuated on occasion by physical outbursts, and her unwillingness to stay in the wheelchair made it impossible for them to take good care of her.

When Lolly asked about other options, they suggested she could/should be moved to the nursing-care wing, where the staff was larger and better equipped to deal with Mom. Unfortunately, there were, they told Lolly, no vacancies right then, so Mom might have to be moved to a nursing home away from the Chelsea Methodist Home until a spot was available for her.

Ray, our stepfather, had been in a nursing home. It was smelly and ugly, and the "care" was questionable. Lolly had worked hard to get him out of the nursing home once she was his legal guardian, but she didn't succeed before he died. She was not anxious to have Mom anywhere but in the Chelsea Methodist Home. She also knew they couldn't move her to another facility without heavily sedating her, which wouldn't be good either. She pushed for other options.

The staff said they might be able to keep Mom on the Alzheimer's wing until a spot in nursing became available if we were able to provide twenty-four-hour private nursing care for her. The cost: $260 a day.

Lolly and I went back and forth on the telephone trying to figure out what to do. Mom only had about $80,000 left in disposable income: the rest was tied up in her house. We quickly realized that at $260 a day, the

$80,000 would cover only 307 days of care: less than a year. Buying private nursing care didn't seem like a viable option.

We were in a catch-22. We had always said we would sell her house to pay for her care, but renting her house did a better job of providing her with an income to pay for her care—as long as the cost of her care remained around $35,000 a year. The rent from her house, Ray's pension, and the small pension Mom got from our father, along with her social security check, were, until now, covering most of her expenses. We were prepared to sell her house, but selling the house had some strings attached.

We still hadn't finished all the repairs necessary to meet the requirements of the buyer-protection laws in Mom's community. Slowly, over the years of renting it, we had had one repair done after another in preparation for the time we would have to sell it. We had replaced the roof, put in air-conditioning, had the masonry work done, and painted the garage, but we had not done the foundation repairs.

Home repairs are not only costly, they're time consuming. You can schedule a repairman to come, but he comes when he wants to come, which may be six hours, six weeks, or even six months from the time you wanted him there. Consequently, Mom's house was far from easily accessed disposable income.

Lolly was prepared to try negotiating with the staff in the hopes of keeping Mom in the Alzheimer's wing until something became available in nursing. If we could hire a private nurse for the "worst times" of the day rather than around the clock, we might be able to buy Mom a little more time. The last thing we wanted to do was move her twice. A move of any kind would be difficult, but two moves would be a disaster.

Lolly didn't even have a chance to discuss this option. By the next day, Mom had become extremely agitated at the staff's attempts to confine her to a wheelchair, and she kicked and punched several people. In the midst of our nursing-care, what-to-do-with-Mom-now crisis, someone on the nursing floor in the Methodist Home died. Mom was immediately bumped to the top of the "priority list" for this placement and two days later was moved to the medical wing.

It was a tragic way for us to find a solution to our problem. But like so many things with Alzheimer's, all solutions have their strings, downsides, and compromises.

In the wake of these tumultuous two days, I considered dropping everything and going to Michigan. Lolly kept saying no, it was under control. Besides, she insisted there would be worse problems to handle in the future. With Alzheimer's, just when you think you have the situation in hand and you're on smooth ground, providing the best care you can, something new crops up and you're back to square one.

During this period of difficulty with her foot and the subsequent falls, Mom became more agitated and weepy. Through this transition and other changes Mom experienced, my respect for the staff and the "institution" of the Chelsea Methodist Home grew and continues to grow. Through all their difficulties with Mom, they have never once resorted to "snowing" her—the term the nursing staff uses to describe sedating a patient to the point of immobilizing them. Also, the restraints they use on her are minimal.

This does not make the situation easier. We are still left wondering what Mom thinks. We have quit asking her because she cannot tell us. She not only couldn't tell us what was wrong, she couldn't understand what we were trying to ask her. Lolly repeatedly told Mom not to try walking because her foot wouldn't work, not to get out of the chair because she would fall down, and to please stay in the wheelchair so she could remain on Wesley Hall for a while longer. Mom's response was to stand up and try to walk to show Lolly how strong she was. And again, with Lolly watching, she fell. She fell because she didn't understand. Lolly couldn't make her understand.

Still we can't help but wonder if we can do better than we are doing now, fighting to keep her in a place we know is clean, safe, and equipped at all hours of the day and night to both restrain and help her.

The Methodist Home is, undeniably, a form of "restraint." The home confines her movements. It controls her environment. It keeps her from moving freely in the world.

When she lived on the Alzheimer's wing, the elevator

was locked so she couldn't leave. On the medical wing, she wears an alarm system clipped to the back of her wheelchair. It goes off if she leaves the ward, signaling to the nurses that she's escaped.

For the most part, she is unaware of these restraints. They no longer wedge a cloth-covered foam pad in between the front arms of her wheelchair to make it difficult for her to get out of her chair. Instead, they use a seat belt, though she rarely tries to stand since she has lost her sense of balance. Even without her flopping foot, she could not keep herself upright for long.

We are both comfortable and uncomfortable with these restraining devices. We are aware of their necessity but wonder what the lives of the patients would be like without them.

If we had Mom in one of our homes, we would have to use many more forms of restraint to keep her from hurting herself, from hurting us, and from damaging our collective environment. In her present state, where she has lost all reasoning ability, Mom can be destructive to herself, others, and her environment.

One difference we have observed between the Alzheimer's patients and the other geriatric patients on the medical wing is that the Alzheimer's patients are more restless. They scoot their wheelchairs incessantly from one end of the hall to the other. They also propel their walkers and walking devices at an alarming and erratic speed. They are, for the most part, more aggressive than the geriatric residents.

Maybe they need a couple hours every day on an indoor track, racing each other in their various mobility devices, to work off their aggression and agitation. Maybe they need wider halls and bigger spaces to roam. Maybe they need gardens to dig in, little inclines to struggle up with their wheelchairs, windows to open and close, or environmental changes and challenges. Maybe, as their minds wind backward, furiously erasing their memories, their brain motors are racing forward and need some release.

Maybe there are other ways to help Alzheimer's victims spend their last frustrating days rather than continuously modifying existing hospital environments so we might keep these patients more contained.

At present what is available for Alzheimer's victims is a "medical" model consistent with old age and geriatric needs. This model is filled with wheelchairs, feeding tubes, adult diapers, bedpans, and medication. It is in many ways an appropriate and decent model. But I can't help wishing that there were a better one.

11

THE PHYSICAL DECLINE

It's October 13, 1994, Lolly's birthday. Mom's birthday is October 17, and I dread it. When I saw her in August, she kept asking if it was her birthday. No, she kept insisting it was her birthday.

My sleep has been flooded with nightmares of her birthday and her death. In my dreams they are the same. The dream feels like a car wreck where my rib cage has been jerked too hard and the wind knocked out of me. I often wake up crying and unable to breathe.

My mother used to say she was psychic. It is the only trait I got from her. I do not have her black hair, broad cheekbones, or hazel eyes. I have instead an uneasy ability to feel the future: a twisted gift to sense what is happening before it happens. But knowing she is going to die takes no gift.

We are beginning to see the first signs of her physical decline. She is a little herky-jerky when she tries to move or hold things. She can't walk without assistance. Her speech pattern has also changed, signaling some new damage in her brain. She gets stuck on sounds, stuttering them out in an odd cadence: "Dodo-do-do yo-yo-you want to-to-to-to go."

She, like all of us, will die. It is difficult, however, despite the rampant destruction of her brain, to predict when or how she will die. The nagging suspicion that hers will not be a swift and merciful death, however, is our greatest concern. As each new manifestation of her decline comes forward, we are even more aware of how uncomfortable her life with this disease must be. Each new "symptom" is greeted with a rising agitation from her, making her more and more difficult to handle and hold.

When I was shopping with a friend one Saturday morning, we stumbled on an artist's yard sale. The artist's front porch was full of handmade baskets, quilts, and dolls that she had made and wanted to be rid of in order to make her life more manageable.

My mother used to love dolls. This woman's dolls were soft and touchable. I was having a hard time looking at them, thinking about how, if my mother were well, if she were herself, she would love being on this woman's lawn, touching her dolls, taking time to make the best selection, find the prettiest one to buy and take home.

That's when I found the teddy bear. It was on the ground surrounded by dolls and miniature baskets. It was a patchwork teddy bear, with a barrel of a tummy, and it was soft, so soft you could sense the years of loving in it. It was made from an old blue-and-white quilt that had been touched and washed so many times, it was nearly threadbare.

I bought it, brought it home, changed its startled blue button eyes to soft brown ones, tied one blue and one white satin ribbon around its neck, wrapped it in tissue, and sent it to my sister to give to my mother. I hoped if Lolly took it to her, Mom might understand it was a present: hers to keep and hold and talk to.

Mom would get candy, flowers, and a teddy bear for her birthday. Ironically, Lolly would spend her own birthday meeting with the Chelsea Methodist Home's medical staff to discuss Mom's condition. Every ninety days, Lolly has to meet with the staff to review Mom's "case."

The nursing wing is a medical wing, and when they moved her from the Alzheimer's unit to the medical wing, they did a complete workup on Mom. These medical tests revealed Mom had, in addition to Alzheimer's, extreme hardening of the arteries in the brain, high blood pressure, and emphysema from years of smoking.

There was some speculation regarding her inability to walk, and some suspicion that this inability stemmed from a stroke rather than from nerve damage, as they had originally thought. Hypertension in combination with hardening of the arteries in the brain is an invitation for strokes to occur.

None of this should have been surprising. The natural course of aging produces hardening of the arteries in the brain, and the resulting high blood pressure would make sense. The chronic pulmonary condition could have been predicted from her many years of smoking.

There was, however, something awful for me in knowing these additional diagnoses. Before this medical meeting, I felt like all we were battling here was Alzheimer's.

I was shocked to realize I still held on to the hope that she would recover and be whole enough to go out shopping with me on a Saturday morning, cruising yard sales, buying dolls, talking and laughing. But I did, because it's hard, even in the face of reason, to give up hope. Mom was still alive. She was still my mother. And my mother used to do those things.

For Lolly, the meeting with the medical personnel and the additional medical information were a relief. She felt she could at last accept that there was something medically wrong with Mom. For her, Mom was not just mean or crazy anymore, but physically sick.

A terrible ambiguity surrounds Alzheimer's. Despite the number of physical and psychological tests used to reach the tentative conclusion someone might have Alzheimer's, you're always left wondering if the doctors might be wrong in their diagnosis. They are the first to admit that the only *real* test for the disease is an autopsy.

So you wonder if your loved one really does have Alzheimer's, or if the doctors have missed something. Maybe it isn't Alzheimer's at all, but a brain tumor, a vitamin deficiency, or some psychotic behavior that could easily be cured with a miracle drug like Prozac. Worse yet, you are left wondering if your mother isn't just a hateful old person who doesn't remember the good times or anything about her life or yours. The bottom line in all of this is that you fear somehow that you've all failed to see the truth.

The new knowledge I now had—that my mother possessed some real physical quirks and manifestations of both normal aging and Alzheimer's—felt like a burden. The truth had at last been revealed: she could die from Alzheimer's, probably from some failure to swallow, drowning in her own spit, and she could also have a stroke and die. In fact, she had probably had a small stroke already.

The knowledge made me feel responsible. What were we to do with this knowledge? Demand preventive medication? But what medication? Why? Have them alter her diet? To what? Something that lessened the hardening of the arteries in the brain? Something that would humanely speed the process? More chocolate, less chocolate, red wine, champagne?

We had once believed it would be a blessing if Mom had a stroke. Knowing that it was a possibility, it no longer felt like a blessing. It felt confusing and awful and frightening. Mom does not know what is happening to her. I can't imagine how they even managed to calm her enough to get a blood sample from her or fasten a blood pressure cuff around her arm.

I thought of a friend whose mother had recently died of cancer. She knew her mother was dying. Her mother knew she was dying, and together they planned a trip. It was a physically and emotionally hard trip. But it was something they did together.

My mother and I cannot sit and make plans together. We cannot take a trip. We can't even cruise around some sunny Saturday afternoon looking for yard sales.

My brothers and sister and I visit. We wait. We talk to Mom and listen to her and wonder if she knows she is losing bits and pieces of her mind. We worry she knows she is slowly being ravaged and destroyed by something, most probably Alzheimer's.

There was an article in the paper the other day about a local bluegrass performer who has bowed out of the concert circuit because he has Alzheimer's. I read the article with fascination. He clearly and lucidly described the episodes of memory loss that he was experiencing: the blankness, the inability to call up lyrics he had sung for more than twenty years, the hardship of putting a name and a face together on a friend, the struggle to remember what song he had just played.

After reading the article, I wanted to ask Mom if she had these experiences. I wanted to know what it felt like for her. But I can't ask because she doesn't know. She isn't able to remember, and she never told us anything about how she felt until it was too late.

The week before, in a different article, a daughter recounted her mother's insistence, before it was discovered she had Alzheimer's, that she didn't want to hear anything bad. Mom did a similar thing. From about 1989 on, she didn't want to hear anything bad about our lives, but she became fascinated with grisly murders and cut out articles from the paper and carried them around in her purse. Once when the children and I were sitting on the floor playing with blocks in Lolly's family room, Mom came in, sat down, opened her purse, and began reading aloud from one of these articles. When I tried to tell her I thought the incident was terrible but not appropriate for the children to hear, she got mad and stormed out of the room. We were unable to talk about what she was thinking, why she had read the article to me, why she carried it in her purse, or what she was afraid of or angry about.

We have no evidence that she ever had a time when she knew what was happening to her and could think about what it meant. We are left believing she never had the chance to make plans or decisions for the rest of her life, as this bluegrass player did. She never talked to us about what she felt or what she wanted.

Knowing her body is poised to have a stroke at any moment saddens me in a deep and disturbing way. It doesn't seem right. None of this seems right. A stroke seems violent, a last wrenching of life. Let her sleep. Let her dream. Let her remember for a minute in the dream that she was once alive. Let her have a moment of peace slipping from one life to another.

12

THE DISTANCE
BETWEEN OUR LIVES

Early in the fall of 1994, we decided we would be on our own for Thanksgiving but would go up to Michigan to see Mom for Christmas. Jeff and I also decided we didn't want to drive from North Carolina to Michigan in the winter. It is, even in the best of weather, a long drive, and neither of us finds driving a relaxing sport.

When we started to make plane reservations, the kids protested. They didn't want to fly. They weren't afraid of flying, but they also weren't in favor of flying. We couldn't understand why, so we talked about it. After several dinner discussions about the joys of driving versus flying, it came out that the children felt flying was too abrupt, too sudden a wrenching from here to there. When I thought about it, I agreed.

It is hard to go "from here to there." The distance from our lives to Mom's is an ever more difficult and distant journey. We didn't need transportation as much as we needed a way to ease into her life.

We settled on taking the train. We took full advantage of our travel mode, using our five-hour layover in Washington, D.C., to go to the National Gallery's East Wing for lunch and a walk through both the Toulouse-Lautrec and the Milton Avery shows before reboarding the train in time to make dinner reservations in the dining car. It is the most civilized way to travel.

Shortly after we pulled into Ann Arbor the next morning, we took Lolly to work and the kids to see Mom.

Mom was in the dining area of the medical wing eating lunch when we arrived. It was the first time we had been to see her since she had been moved two and a half months earlier.

Although clean and well cared for, the medical unit is not as visually appealing as Wesley Hall, the Alzheimer's wing. The halls are wider and barer in order to accommodate wheelchairs. The nurses' station is located at the center of the wing, and there's more medical support equipment, quietly signaling that people here are impaired. Almost everyone is in a wheelchair or uses some sort of walking device. Most of the residents need assistance in eating, so mealtimes are messy and take forever.

The overall impact of seeing Mom sitting alone in a wheelchair, a tray table with her lunch pulled close to her chair so she could work through trying to feed herself, while all around her, adults wearing big bibs were being spoon-fed by attendants, was upsetting. Lolly had said we would be shocked. The need for the wheelchair had dramatically changed Mom's appearance. Her inability to move had robbed her of some of her fire. She didn't look up when we approached.

It took several minutes before she realized we were standing there speaking to her. Even then, she did not immediately respond to us or realize we were there for her.

When I sat down next to her to talk with her face to face, I noticed she was holding a doll. When I mentioned the doll, she stopped eating, took the doll in both hands, and held it out at arm's length and began talking to it.

She talked, cooed, whistled, and made faces at the doll, rocking it back and forth so its eyes opened and closed. Then she brought it close to her and held it on her shoulder like a baby and resumed eating. We stayed with her in the dining room until she finished her lunch, then wheeled her out into the hall.

The dining room made me uncomfortable. I wanted to get out of there. Also, the youngest children, Cole and Colin, were proving dangerous with all the walkers and wheelchairs around, so we asked the attendant at the nurses' station if we could take Mom off the ward for a walk. She said yes and explained that Mom had on an alarm band, so we would need to trip the alarm device near the door in order to get out.

Getting out was not so easy. Mom, although she was in a wheelchair, was situated so her feet were resting on the floor. By shuffling her feet, she could propel the wheelchair forward and backward. She could also put her feet down stubbornly and stop you from moving her.

After some cajoling, coaxing, and gentle pushing, we got her going forward. Neil, our oldest son, took charge of pushing Mom off the ward into the other areas of the building. Jeff, the other kids, and I kept chatting away, pointing out all the pretty pictures and flowers to her as we moved along so we could keep her going through the halls.

It took a while, but we finally moved through the building to the new wing, where there is a sunny common seating area and an ice cream parlor. The ice cream parlor is run by volunteer residents who open it each afternoon from two to four, serving malts, shakes, sundaes, and sodas at minimal cost.

While we were waiting for the shop to open, we moved around the big sunny lobby area looking at the various Christmas decorations, trying to engage Mom in conversation. It was clear that her language skills had declined, but she was oddly happier than we had seen her before. The doll seemed to calm her, and from time to time, she would take it from her shoulder and make faces at it, cooing and whistling, the way we all do when we are holding newborn babies.

By the time we finished our ice cream and maneuvered our way through the halls back to her new home, I was exhausted. It was a struggle to establish and maintain "contact" with her. I felt as if she had slipped even farther away from us than she had been just the day before. It was as though she had lost even more than fine motor control, memory, or language. It felt as though she had lost some essential part of her self.

The ancient Greeks believed the body had humors. Although the idea seems more mystically than medically sound, I sometimes wonder if the Greeks were right. And if so, perhaps Alzheimer's not only robs its victims of memories but of humors as well. What it felt like that day was that her disease had tired of just robbing her of memory and had, instead, boldly moved forward and robbed her of one of her essential humors. Even more horrifying was the thought that perhaps the disease had drained all it could from her memory and was now working its way through her soul.

It was a chilling thought. As I struggled to engage her, I felt as though I were also struggling to maintain my own precarious sanity.

The next day. We left the kids at home, so Lolly and I could go alone to visit Mom. When we got there, Mom seemed agitated, distracted, and unfocused. I noticed that all the patients were parked in the hallway and two nurses were working their way from one end of the ward to the other. One of them approached us.

"The doll is gone," she said, as though we knew what she was talking about. "We can't find her doll. The doll really helps her. Did she have it when you came back yesterday?"

She did. I had a sudden chilling fear that the doll might be her last connection with the world. Yes, the doll is important. We took Mom down the hall to her room. Calmly and methodically, we searched the place. We checked drawers, under the bed, the closet, the bathroom, the trash can, the little bookcase, behind the pillows in her chair. She had lost other things, including her glasses, her teeth, and numerous purses and favorite gaudy necklaces. Many of these items have never been found, which makes me wonder if Alzheimer's doesn't have something to do with the mysterious black holes of the universe.

In our search, we took the time to look through her clothes. They were looking pretty laundry abused and shopworn. We decided we needed to buy her some new things. Pretty things to make her look nice. We didn't find the doll.

Before we came, we had stopped by Mom's favorite bakery and bought her three jelly doughnuts. When we got to her room and she saw the box, like a child, her eyes lit up and she became excited. When we gave the box to her, she opened it and started in on them. She was delighted and enthusiastically licked jelly off her fingers as she moved from one doughnut to the next. The sugar from the doughnuts got everywhere, and when we cleaned her up, washing her hands and face, and brushed the crumbs from her clothes, we took the opportunity to brush her hair, clean her up a little special. I enjoyed the brief moment of doing and fussing, washing a small spot from her clothes, making her look nice. It was one of the only moments I have had recently where I felt as though being there with her mattered.

We stayed and visited for nearly two hours. Mostly we sat with her, trying, when we could, to pick up and respond to what she was attempting to say. We told her about her brothers and sisters and read their messages to her on the Christmas cards she'd gotten, but when we asked her if she remembered her siblings, she got distracted and visibly upset. I felt guilty that we have never told her that two of her sisters, Alice and Nedra, have died. We decided not to tell because we were afraid it would upset her and confuse her. It is hard to know the right thing to do anymore.

The staff still hadn't found the doll by the time we left. So we told them we'd go out and buy another one. The nurse at the desk brightened. "It's a help, really a help," she said, punctuating her words with her hands. She told us Mom doesn't cry as much when she has the doll.

"The doll," she said, her face hopeful that we'd find what Mom needed, "has to have hair, and eyes that open and shut when you lay it down and pick it up, and hands"—she held her hands out like a child's—"that are curved, like this, with the fingers open. She tries to put things in the doll's hands, to feed it. And a nice face. The doll should have a nice face."

We left the hospital to go shopping. It was Christmas

Eve. We still had stockings to fill, presents to wrap, and dinner to cook. We were also painfully aware that we might not find this doll this late and so close to Christmas.

We went to a local discount store and worked our way down the toy aisle, picking up boxes to see if eyes opened and shut. We found a few dolls left on the shelves, some with hair, some without. We chose the prettiest ones with hair and took them out of their boxes to test them. We knew a good doll had to be soft and easy to hold.

We quickly rejected two with nice faces and fairly decent heads of hair because they were hard and felt cold to the touch. We checked the hands and found a couple with nicely curled fingers and open palms.

In the end, we settled on a classic: a blond-haired, blue-eyed Betsy Wetsy with a wide face and smile. It's a good doll. She was dressed in a short top, matching booties, diaper, and rubber pants. She had a comb and brush and a bottle. When you filled the bottle with water, it could be fed to the doll, and as the name implied, this water worked its way down to a wet diaper. The doll looked a lot like the one she lost. We thought she'd like it.

Christmas Day. The kids are up early. The little ones are so excited by their stockings, they don't even notice the unwrapped "Santa" presents waiting under the tree.

Chuck came Christmas Eve and had dinner and then

spent the night. It is fun having him here, like a big kid, waiting for Christmas. The kids have made a stocking for him filled with dozens of wrapped screwdrivers and small tools that Lolly and Tom bought for him. They have fun watching him unwrap them.

We take our time opening the presents in turns, unwrapping the gifts one at a time, stopping on occasion to assemble something and play with it.

Once the gifts are undone and the paper is cleaned up, we go to the kitchen and work a little on the dinner preparations. With the turkey in the oven, we get ready to go see Mom.

It will be the first Christmas we don't bring her home. It feels odd and uncomfortable. The wheelchair and her lack of mobility, coupled with her growing unpredictability, have made it not only unwieldy but also unwise to bring her home.

Colin is undone by all the excitement and desperate for a nap, so we leave Lolly and Colin at home when we go. It is cold outside, but there isn't even a hint of snow: another sign Christmas isn't right this year.

I'm surprised by how few cars there are in the parking lot at the Methodist Home. I would have thought there would be lots of families visiting or many of the residents gone. But neither is true. It feels like a regular day on the floor. Everyone is present and accounted for and cruising along in their wheelchairs and walkers.

We look for Mom but can't find her at first because

she is still eating lunch in the dining area. We wait while she finishes, then take her to the hall. A nurse sees us carrying presents and pushing Mom. She ushers us into a private sitting room and says we should feel free to close the doors and stay there for as long as we like. There don't seem to be too many other families looking for places to visit.

The kids take off their coats and pile them up on a chair. They are anxious for Mom to unwrap her presents, for her to see her doll. It feels like Christmas for them again, but it takes Mom a long time to understand that she is supposed to unwrap the presents the children give her. Cole is dancing around in front of her, jiggling with excitement. He loves to help unwrap presents but always wants to try to save the paper. The wrapping paper has reindeer leaping across a field of bright red and holly. The present is tied with dozens of curled ribbons. Mom touches the bow as if the bow were her present. Cole can't wait any longer and shows her where the tape is easiest to pull off.

When the doll is uncovered, Mom seems pleased but disconcerted: it is trapped in the box. We pull it out to find it is held in place by long twist ties, and we work as fast as we can to get them undone, because she is upset that the doll can't move.

When I finally get the doll out, she won't look at it or take it. The kids are upset by her reaction and try to tell her the baby doll is hers. When she finally takes the doll in her hands, she tips it so its eyes open and close. She talks baby talk to it, whistles to it, and makes odd clucking noises.

It is scary to witness your mother go through these gestures. Chuck has pulled away from the group and is sitting back watching, tears rolling down his face.

We stay for about two hours, combing the doll's hair, talking to Mom, sitting with her, showing her the little plastic baby bottle so she can feed her doll.

Cole and Hedy wonder what the body of the doll looks like and try to take its clothes off. Mom waves her hands at them and warns them to be careful.

We are very careful. The day feels fragile, fractured, nearly destroyed. When it seems as though all the air has been sucked from the room we have been sitting in, we get our coats and start to go. We bring Mom out in the hall to say good-bye and let the nurse know we are going. Mom holds her doll on her shoulder, lifting it up from time to time to blow in its face, whistling at it, making its eyes blink as she rocks its body back and forth. The kids hug her and kiss her good-bye.

When we go down the hall, she tries to follow us. The nurse from the front desk comes to see the doll, to help us leave. Unexpectedly, as she is moving Mom down the hall, the nurse calls out to us, "Why wouldn't she want to follow you?" I feel scalded by her words, reproached for not being a good enough daughter to take my mother home for Christmas dinner.

We do not talk about Mom at all after we leave. Balancing our "well" lives against our mother's disease-riddled one is a terrible strain.

The day after Christmas. We need a mission, a purpose, so we dress to brave the biggest shopping/exchange day of the year to go in search of new things for Mom to wear. It feels like an adventure, a welcome release from a scary claustrophobic time.

Lolly has to work, so Tom, Jeff, and I have the kids. Neil and Quentin want to wander off on their own at the mall, which is fine. Tom and Jeff offer to take the two little ones exploring while Hedy and I shop for Mom.

We go to Lane Bryant. Mom, although she's smaller than she used to be, is still on the big side. We have to guess at her clothing size.

The wheelchair presents a number of clothing problems. Mom likes jackets and vests, but if they're too long, they're hard to sit in and wind up bunching up in the back and just being so much twisted material.

Everything is on sale and we decide to do it up right, getting her matching slacks and tops, a vest she can wear with several things, new pajamas, and a robe.

Hedy and I have fun picking colors, matching outfits, and imagining what Mom would have picked out on her own. We talk about things looking "like Grandma" and find things she might have thought were too expensive but would make her look smart. We are conscious we want her to look her best, to look like she is loved. We buy only those things we think are beautiful.

We pick the softest and prettiest long terrycloth robe we can find. The "tub" room is off the entrance hall of the ward. We want her to look good when she's in the hall waiting for her bath. We want her to feel wrapped up and warm when she finishes.

We are pleased with our purchases. When we go to visit her later in the afternoon, we give them not to her but to the attendant at the nurses' station so her name labels can be sewn into them, marking them for the laundry. The attendant remarks on how many things we've bought. We tell her we want Mom to look nice. When the tags are in, we'll go through her closet and get rid of those things too worn to be nice anymore.

The wheelchairs and walkers of the medical wing work to reduce these residents to the category of patient. The shift of person to patient robs them all of some of their identity. The wealth of clothes we have purchased for Mom seems as extreme to the attendant as it seems necessary to me. I want Mom to look great, to be a bit of sparkle in this otherwise drab existence. If she sparkles, maybe she'll be noticed more. Maybe someone will stop and compliment her, smile at her, and make her feel like a person instead of a patient.

Again, we take Mom and the kids for a walk through halls of the complex and go "out" for ice cream. Everyone gets malts, including Mom, and the kids show her how to suck it up with a straw. She stops several times while she is drinking to tell them it's good. She loves ice cream.

There is another family "out" for ice cream. They recognize Mom and say hello. Their mother is a patient on the Alzheimer's wing, Wesley Hall. They ask how it is where Mom is now. We tell them the truth. We tell them it's nice, but not as nice as Wesley Hall. There's nothing else to say.

When we walk back through the building, we stop in the music room. Both Neil and Hedy sit down and play the organ for her. Because the organ faces a wall, their backs are facing her when they sit to play. Mom gets confused by the sound and doesn't realize they are playing for her.

When Neil is finished and Hedy takes her turn at the keyboard, Mom moves a little in her chair to watch what she is going to do. "Beautiful hands she has," Mom says, pointing at Hedy. It is the most appropriate and complete sentence she has made during the visit. Hedy does have beautiful hands, and Mom's statement catches me unprepared and makes me choke a little.

On our way back to Mom's room, we see an attendant from Wesley Hall. She stops to talk to Mom and to ask us how she's doing. We tell her she's declined. She says she's heard. She touches Mom's hand and tells her she misses her. I tell her it's all very sad, and she agrees.

* * *

December 27. Colin and Quentin decide to stay home, so Jeff and I just take Neil, Hedy, and Cole to see Mom. Lolly has to go to work again but suggests we take something to the hospital with us to "play" with Mom. She had tried the other week to color with her in a coloring book and had some success and thinks it might be good if we can get her to do something with her hands.

We decide on Play-Doh, so we stop at a couple of stores on our way to the Methodist Home. The shelves were pretty much picked clean by Christmas. The only thing I find is a Play-Doh finger-puppet kit, so I buy it.

When we get to Mom's, things feel rocky. She doesn't recognize us and is very agitated we have come. She points at the kids and asks why they are there. I'm apprehensive about staying, but I don't know what else to do. At least with the Play-Doh in hand, the kids will have something to keep them busy while I try to talk with her and calm her.

Neil keeps trying to engage her with the Play-Doh, but she keeps pushing him away and saying, "No, no." I am playing with Neil and Hedy, pressing Play-Doh into the puppet forms around their fingers, making little finger puppets of Elmo, Cookie Monster, Bert, and Ernie. Mom holds her doll close to her, stroking the back of its head, talking to it, holding it up above her head, and telling it what a good baby it is, one that has never given her trouble. I wish I knew what was going on in her mind.

I try to talk with Mom for a minute, then when I turn back to the kids and the Play-Doh, I realize Neil is gone. I get a little scared. I didn't see him go and hope he is all right. When he comes back, he doesn't come into the room but stands in the doorway.

He tells me he has heard someone playing the violin. Neil has played the violin since he was in third grade. He asks if he can find where the music is coming from. I tell him it's fine.

When he comes back, he is very excited. There's a man playing the violin in the dining room. He wants to take Mom. We gather up the Play-Doh and puppet forms and put them back into the box. Then we take Mom down the hall to hear the music.

The attendants are wheeling people into the dining room. There's a woman playing the piano and a man strolling around the room playing a violin. One of the residents is clapping his hands and singing. The others sit and listen and watch or doze.

When the man stops, Neil approaches him and asks if he can borrow his violin for a moment. The man hands it to him, and Neil faces Mom and starts to play. He plays bits and pieces from his recent recital and a few pieces he has performed with his orchestra at middle school. Neil is good and has always played in a way you don't expect a child to play, as though it is part of his heart. The man is surprised, even more surprised when he finds out our six-foot-one Neil is only thirteen.

For the next forty-five minutes, Neil and the man, a local Methodist minister who comes every week to play for them, take turns playing. It is a natural and easy exchange, with the violin trading hands every couple of songs. A gentleman in a wheelchair nearest the piano claps his hands loudly and sings while the others sit and watch.

Once or twice Mom looks at Neil when he plays. The look is more puzzling than praising. She seems unsure the music is coming from him. She watches him, then looks away, then turns back and watches again, but mostly she fiddles with her doll and strokes its hair.

When it's time for us to leave, Mom fusses a little with the doll, straightening her clothes and moving her arms. The kids take turns touching Mom and saying good-bye. Mom doesn't attempt to follow us this time and, in fact, hardly notices when we go.

December 29. We take a brief "vacation" day in Lansing, playing with the kids at the hands-on science museum, the Oldsmobile museum, and the newly refurbished state capitol. It is just the break we need to get our balance back and believe we are a family again.

December 30. Now that Mom is on a medical unit, care meetings are scheduled every ninety days for the staff to report to the family. Since it is time for another meeting, we go ahead and schedule one so both Lolly and I can attend.

The meetings are held off the ward in a conference room on the first floor. One of the nurses attends as well as the program director. Although the meeting is supposed to be informal and purely for information purposes, my stomach feels as though we have been called to the principal's office.

At Lolly's first meeting, she had to sign off on the level of care we wanted for Mom: in other words, how much medical intervention we wanted on Mom's behalf. By law, the options have to be reviewed during each care meeting. Again we choose "Code A," indicating we want Mom to be comfortable; if necessary, she should be treated with antibiotics for infections and narcotics for pain; we do not want her transferred to an intensive care setting; and we want no aggressive treatment or life supports. We have not changed our thinking. Without any hesitation, all four of us, her children, have agreed that this is what she would want, but having to review the options again, this time in the context of a medical unit, is creepy. It didn't feel as bad when we had to make the decision on Wesley Hall. We had a sense when she was there that she was going to be fine, that nothing would harm her.

I remind myself, over and over again in my head, this is what I would want for myself. In fact, I wonder sometimes if we have already done too much with the seemingly benign yet gentle intervention of placing her in the care of the Methodist Home. I don't know anymore if I would want to live at all without a mind. I do not know if I could live half knowing, half not knowing that my children would have to watch me deteriorate memory by memory, capability by capability. When I think of my mother's present life, I feel the urge to live dangerously, take risks, drink a tad more champagne than is good for me, eat chocolate, and hope that if I am genetically destined to get Alzheimer's, I will get lucky enough to die from some foolishness devised by my own hand, full of life, not drained of it.

The meeting feels uncomfortably serious. The staff is thorough and caring. They review Mom's blood pressure, her recent weight gain, her charted problems of cerebral arteriosclerosis, hypertension, pulmonary problems from years of smoking cigarettes, and her recent change and increase of medication. She is now on Paxil and Mellaril, antidepressant and antianxiety drugs, and seems to be responding better. They mention the doll and note they are unsure what is responsible for her recent move from deep depression to manageable depression: the drugs or the doll, or the two in tandem.

They talk about her meeting her "goals." I want to giggle but suppress the urge. Mom hasn't got a clue that she has "goals" she is expected to meet. The staff, however, is quite serious about these goals, and although the idea seems silly, I realize these goals keep the staff focused on her care, keep them encouraged and working to help her. I am grateful they can hold tight to such an idea.

One completed goal they discuss with pride is reducing her crying to two hours or less a day. My heart is drained at the prospect that crying two hours or less a day would be a desirable goal, and I want to cry myself. They are thrilled to report she has reached her goal and, with the help of the doll, no longer sits outside the director's office crying all day.

We ask about visiting her. We want to know if it helps. We are looking less for the truth than a reassurance that we are doing something right or need to do it more often, because we are so unsure ourselves. Sometimes it feels right. Sometimes it feels awful. She is unable to verbalize how she feels, and we leave not knowing if our coming has been good or bad. More often than not, we are at an emotional loss as to what we should do, and we are embarrassed by our lack of knowledge and understanding regarding what is good for our mother.

Oddly enough, the staff shifts in their chairs a little: they are the ones uncomfortable with the question. The truth: since we have been visiting every day this week, Mom has been more difficult, more agitated and volatile. There have been a couple of incidents, difficult times for the staff, when she has lashed out. Morally it is right to visit, but management-wise it is difficult if we come. My head spins. I have lost some thread that ties us to the reality of what a family is and what constitutes relationships and responsibilities.

We ask, remembering the comment that the staff member made to us regarding Mom's desire to follow us out the door, if we should try to take her out again. The idea sounds like a good one, but on second thought, the staff is unsure how long Mom can be gone and not become confused and overwhelmed, scared and violent.

I am beginning to understand the security of staying with "goals," of focusing on things like blood pressure, weight gain and loss, and medicine dosage. Pressed with anything so weighty as obligation and relationship, we snap like taut rubberbands and begin to focus on maintenance details: they've added side rails to her bed, she needs to have some minor medical procedures and tests done, and we have to sign papers approving IV sedation.

I mention noticing there is always a carton of milk on her meal tray. I tell them Mom has never in her life willingly drunk a glass of milk. I tell them I suspect she is lactose intolerant and want it noted in her chart. If they force her to drink milk, she'll have trouble with her stomach and will also become unwilling to eat and will wind up having to be force-fed: something we want to avoid. I make the observation on her behalf, hoping to gain some dignity for her. I don't like milk either and can't imagine being forced to drink it every day.

The nurse stiffens. She wants to know how I propose Mom will get her daily calcium requirement. I suggest she can get it through puddings, cheese, ice cream, or even calcium tablets.

Since we brought it up, the nurse wants to discuss our

taking Mom to the ice cream parlor. During her last medical workup, they discovered her cholesterol is elevated. I cannot keep myself from blurting out that most postmenopausal women have elevated cholesterol. The nurse ignores me and continues her lecture.

She notes Mom has gained ten pounds in the past three months. We note she lost forty in the previous two years, during which time she was agitated, active, and prowling the halls. Since she is now confined to a wheelchair, we suggest a ten-pound weight gain would seem natural.

While she's at it, the nurse says she doesn't want us to bring Mom jelly doughnuts anymore. She wants us to substitute jelly beans instead. I bite my tongue.

While we sit ever so still, the nurse waxes on about low-fat sweet options, cholesterol, and high-blood-pressure problems. She has become the guardian of Mom's glowing health. She cannot see the forest for the trees: there is no earthly reason to deny Mom anything, not ice cream, jelly doughnuts, chocolate, or if she asked for it, salted peanuts, beer, and cigarettes.

Lolly and I look at each other and know there is no need to pursue this line of reasoning. We do not need to argue with the staff over their lack of insight into this disease. The ice cream and doughnuts will continue.

I change the subject and mention we want to have Mom's eyes examined. We are worried she might be developing cataracts again. Her right eye is tearing pretty much all the time. The first time she had the cataracts removed, they were diagnosed as "juvenile." We were told the "adult" variety might develop later. We also want her to be seen by a dentist. We want a new set of false teeth made to replace the ones she lost.

The director and the nurse make a note in their charts and begin to talk about scheduling appointments. The nurse seems satisfied to have something to add to her set of goals and objectives.

"This is good," she says. "These things should be done, need to be done. After all, your mother is only seventy-five. She could easily live another fifteen or twenty years."

I feel the impact of her statement like a truck hitting me broadside. My sister puts her hand on the edge of the table to steady herself.

Fifteen or twenty more years. I cannot, and do not, hear anything else that is said. When the meeting is over, my sister and I get up and go in silence. It's time to meet the kids, Jeff, and Tom and then go upstairs to see Mom.

We meet them coming in the door and go up the elevator together. Mom is in the dining room sitting with her friend, Penny. Penny has a new doll, too, and the two of them are sitting at a table, jabbering, and playing with their dolls. An attendant comes in with one of those mechanical parrots with a tape recorder inside that repeats what you say. She uses it to help the patients with their language skills. The kids have fun playing with it. Mom and Penny watch intently, holding on to their dolls.

While we are visiting, a sermon begins to be broadcast

over the loudspeakers. It is Friday afternoon, an odd time for a sermon, and we listen curiously. We quickly realize we are listening to a funeral service for one of the residents, who must have died over Christmas.

The attendants are wheeling in residents. We don't know if they are bringing them into the dining room to get them ready to eat lunch or to listen to the service. The kids have quit playing with the parrot and are focused on the broadcast. I do not want them listening. I do not want them thinking about dying this Christmas. I do not want them to be burdened any longer with the weight of all these damaged lives at the Methodist Home, or of their grandmother whom they adore who is falling apart, falling out of life, out of their lives, without a chance or a clue.

I hear the declaration of the nurse ringing in my ears: *"She could live another fifteen to twenty years."*

The broadcast is too cruel, too bizarre. We wheel Mom out of the dining room, down the hall to her room in order to get away from the broadcast. We all need to escape.

We fuss a little over Mom in her room and comb her hair. We look out the window and talk about the possibility of snow. We tell Mom we will come back in the spring, when the flowers are coming up, to see her again. She seems connected for a moment.

We walk Mom down to the dining room, hoping we have stayed away long enough for the funeral service to be over. I do not want her to have to eat lunch listening to the service. The room is quiet except for the noise of the patients and the unloading of lunch trays. We do not go in but stay instead in the hallway to say our good-byes. The kids give her hugs. Neil touches her head and says good-bye. I kiss her cheek and try to look at her eye to eye, hoping she'll understand I have to go but will come back soon. Mom doesn't seem to notice we are leaving and takes her doll and begins to coo and whistle at it again.

When we get to the parking lot, the kids go with Tom and Jeff, and Lolly and I get into her car. We don't even try to speak until both doors are firmly closed against the cold.

"Twenty years," Lolly says, her hands braced against the steering wheel. "My life is over."

A dark thick depression begins to take hold. We try to chase it off, laughing about the jelly doughnuts, making a pact that we will never come again without doughnuts in hand.

Mom should have doughnuts. She should have something to look forward to, something that brings her joy. And we should have our lives, but our lives are caught for this moment in time with hers, and we are drowning with her. We can't talk about the things that crash though our minds. We can't bear to say out loud that we believe she is already dead and we need to give up trying to swim with her to shore; that we need to let go of her;

that she would not want to prolong her life if she knew her mind was wasted. We don't have the courage to say that twenty more years like this seems like a black and lifeless eternity.

"I mean it, Carrie," my sister says, starting the car and putting it in reverse. "I'm going to get a gun, and if I get this disease, I'm going to go out into the woods, and I'm going to shoot myself."

When we get home, I cannot tell Jeff what happened during the care meeting. I cannot articulate the sadness, pain, and frustration I feel. Instead, I shut down. I spend the afternoon packing our suitcases. I cannot talk to anyone. I cannot say anything.

When we are in the kitchen, cleaning up from dinner, getting ready to go to the train station, I tell my sister I have spent only three Christmas vacations in my life in my own home. It is the wrong thing to say, but I can't help myself. It is not her fault. She reminds me that I am the one who moved away. She stayed. She lives with this every day.

I am sorry. I am overwhelmed with this burden, this half-life, and feel responsible—for what, I no longer know. I want to make it better. I want to take my sister away, to give her a break. I want my mother to wake up one morning and be well enough to fly to my house and live with me and play with my children.

I want to run away. I want all of this to be done with and gone, and yet I know I can't escape. I also know that even though I will get on a train and ride through the night to get home the next day, I will not be able to get far enough away to have my own life.

I feel selfish and angry. I also feel overwhelmed with all that this disease means for our lives.

13

LISTENING TO EXPERTS

An impassioned young woman in a plain black dress steps up to the podium at the Ninth Annual Joseph and Kathleen Bryan Alzheimer's Disease Research Center Conference. She is the first speaker on the program. She claims she's nervous but looks out into the audience in a self-assured, uncocky way that I will grow to appreciate as the conference unrolls. She's here to tell her mother's story. Her mother, she says, slowing her speech and looking out over our heads to the back of the room, was diagnosed with Alzheimer's two years ago, when she was forty-seven years old.

The shock of her statement jolts us awake. Forty-seven. The number murmurs through the crowd like a strong current, a wave gathering momentum to break. We listen, knowing how the story will unravel, because many people in the crowded room have lived the story, have had the phone calls, watched the decline, struggled with the financial, physical, philosophical, and psychological burden of it all. We know.

She has more to say. She is here for a reason. She wants everyone, every doctor, every researcher, social worker, preacher, teacher, mother, and daughter, to know that her mother was not dumb. She uses the word *dumb* like a hammer as she reels off her mother's academic and career accomplishments. It's an impressive list. Her mother was working as the president of a company when she was diagnosed with Alzheimer's. She's telling her mother's story because she wants to put a stop to the demoralizing, damaging, and blatantly false assumption that both doctors and researchers are working from, that if you have a bright active mind, you won't get Alzheimer's.

I feel the crowd of caretakers wanting to rise to their feet and applaud. The shared sentiment is palpable. There is hope in this room. We are here to share, to learn, and to push the falsehoods aside in order to move forward in this awful business.

Afterward, before we break for lunch, an expert, someone with a string of degrees and a title, gets up and rambles through her identified and published list of risk factors leading to Alzheimer's. There's barely a ripple of dissension when she takes her battery-operated flashlight pointer and circles "lower education" emblazoned on the screen before us, and tells us lower intelligence and lower education are both identified risk factors for Alzheimer's.

We are living in two worlds here: one of research, the other of reality. Someone grumbles over lunch that no one should be allowed to do research unless they have some firsthand experience of what they intend to study. Everyone at the table agrees that even good research done by bright well-meaning people, when done in the abstract, can be wrongheaded.

Despite the discussion at lunch and my own feelings that research often misses the mark of reality, I'm feeling charitable. I am willing to brush off this little misfire of the morning and momentarily suspend judgment against this one researcher's work. I sense there is much to learn from the professionals here.

My mind races in renewed hope when another researcher begins her talk by commenting that she believes the "cure" for Alzheimer's will not be a single treatment but a broad spectrum of treatments, because the disease is a syndrome with multifactorial etiology. She speaks clearly and rationally about not only the tangle in the brain but the tangle of the presenting symptoms and the complexity of addressing individual symptoms without adversely affecting others.

I am caught up in the mental exercise of seeing Alzheimer's as a puzzle, spread out on a table, some of the pieces lying face-down, waiting for someone to turn them over to discover their fit. There is an excitement to this researcher's model that makes me feel like a cure is just sitting there waiting to be found. But before I can cast off my discomfort with how little we presently know and can do about Alzheimer's and enjoy the possibilities this presenter's ideas bring forward in the disease model, another speaker brings me back on course.

He tells the story of a young medical student who had great promise and intelligence. This medical student was sitting at his desk one night studying, while his roommate practiced fencing in the room. At precisely the moment when the medical student turned to watch, the roommate lunged and the tip of his foil went through the medical student's left eye into the memory center of his brain. He was left blinded in one eye and with no short- or long-term memory.

The tragedy of this lost "life" is overwhelming. I grieve quickly and deeply for the hell this young man is left to live in, and shake myself to realize this is the same hell my mother lives in now.

The roller coaster churns on. During the next session, a research physician who is caught up in his own tiny corner of concern pushes the professional care-providers in the group to get signed consent for tube feeding early in the game so there aren't any "five o'clock Friday" emergency orders begging for signatures. Nutrition and weight management are his concerns, and, as he says, "with tube feeding, we can extend these people's lives another three to five years."

My blood pressure skyrockets. I want to scream. Would that young medical student, his lost colleague, want to be tube fed? Would he want another three to five years of not knowing, not remembering, not "living"?

My patience is gone. Now, like my fellow caretakers who grumbled over lunch, I want to put a halt to this conference. Research like this man's has fallen off the track. Someone should dial 911 and ask for the help of a philosopher, a theologian, or an ethicist. We've lost it.

There is an oddly surreal moment during the second day, when Joseph Bryan is brought to the podium in his wheelchair. He is the benefactor of the conference and of the Joseph and Kathleen Bryan Neurobiology Research Building at Duke University. It is his birthday. He is ninety-nine years old, and the flat, blank expression on his face hints that he might have some form of dementia. He has been brought forward for us to sing to him. Someone pushes a cart loaded with a birthday cake ablaze in candles in front of Mr. Bryan.

One of the doctors from the Alzheimer's Disease Research Center at Duke is answering questions from the audience when Joseph Bryan and the cake are wheeled in. The doctor notes Mr. Bryan's entrance with a slight nod of his head but keeps his back to the man and continues talking. Someone from the audience has asked a question regarding a recently published treatment for Alzheimer's that is not one of those under study by Duke's research team. The doctor's answer is snide. He seems to have forgotten, or rudely overlooked, the probability that the woman he is addressing is struggling with the reality that she fits the research "risk" profile. Her voice trembles and cracks when she repeats her question. She is not a doctor or a health professional. She is scared. More than likely, she is the primary caregiver for a parent suffering from Alzheimer's and knows firsthand what hell lies ahead.

The candles continue to burn while the doctor from

Duke talks on. Mr. Bryan sits in his wheelchair, not noticing the candles or the speaker. Mr. Bryan is handsomely dressed. His vacant facial expression indicates he hasn't got a clue why he is here. When we stand to sing "Happy Birthday" to him, he sings along. The doctor who has berated the woman in the audience now blows out the candles for Mr. Bryan. They are trick candles and relight as soon as they are blown out. The doctor laughs and blows again and again until he successfully extinguishes the flames. Mr. Bryan stares out blankly into the audience.

It is one of those horrible times when you are aware that you know both too much and too little. The knowledge is uncomfortable. The situation is grotesque. I wrestle with getting my coat and leaving but decide I have paid for this opportunity to learn something from these experts, these cutting-edge scientists, so I should stay, no matter how uncomfortable I feel right now.

The next session is beyond tedium. I do not blame the speaker but blame myself for staying. The speaker drones on and on about her concerns about weight loss in Alzheimer's patients.

My mother lost weight when she moved to the Alzheimer's wing. It seemed perfectly normal to us. She was eating a balanced diet devoid of her favorites: Doritos, cheeseburgers, fries, malts, Baby Ruths, and jelly doughnuts. She was also pacing the halls day and night. Why shouldn't she lose weight?

When she lost control of her right foot and had to use

a wheelchair, she began gaining weight. This also seemed natural. All of a sudden, an active, almost hyperactive adult became sedentary, and her diet didn't change, so she gained weight.

I have no patience with this presentation and the researcher's silly scientific niggling. I stay through lunch to say good-bye to some of the people I have met, then beg off with the excuse that I have to pick up the kids from the baby-sitter.

The packet of materials I have gathered from this conference consumes me. I feel as though my mother is with me, watching over my shoulder, looking through the papers as I read through them, looking for some cure or some relief from her pain. She is in my dreams and my waking thoughts. She pushes her way through the graphs and fancy projections of the probability of getting Alzheimer's. I can almost feel her hand grappling with the papers, trying to find the part of her that is missing.

She is in pain. It doesn't matter to her that anyone else might get this disease. It doesn't matter to her what the risk factors are or the probable causes. She is looking for more than a cure. She is looking for a balm, a way to ease her pain, to retrieve what she has lost, and to think clearly again.

There are times now when I feel my mind has gone with hers. If her memory is lost, then so is my past. If her future cannot be grasped, than mine cannot be either. We are tied by more than DNA and gene pools: we are tied by love, by history, by strong cords and bonds. She is my mother, and I am her daughter. This obviously means more than these researchers have found.

The pathology of this disease is secondary to its path of destruction. We are, however, unable to realize the full impact of the destruction because of the clever packaging: old age. Which is precisely the reason the stories of the forty-seven-year-old mother and the medical student are so important. They are the "humanizing" stories of the disease. The shock of the realization that people who are not at the end of their lives but in the middle—and therefore should, like everyone else who has a future, have a memory—can and do get Alzheimer's, should shake us into thinking in new ways.

The medical student clears my mind. I try to visualize him when I think of my mother and what is best for her. The medical student cannot study or learn because he cannot remember what he has read. Likewise, movies make no sense. Friendships seem out of reach, because there is no recognition, no memory of past conversations or connections. A love relationship is almost impossible to imagine. As I try to use him as a model to understand what is happening to my mother, a question nags at me: Does his lack of memory make him an imbecile?

Is memory intelligence? If it is, what is life like without intelligence?

As my mother loses mobility, the response seems obvious: put her in a wheelchair. But what about her mind?

We do not have wheelchairs for minds. We have no artificial means to propel memory along or to make up for what is missing in someone's brain. Is there some computer aid we need to explore? Some memory tricks we haven't tried yet?

My mother is agitated and depressed. These are the kinds of symptoms the medical professionals know how to treat: they medicate. They tried Prozac and a number of other drugs and finally hit on some combination to help her contain herself better. But only better. She is not normal. She is not happy.

How can she be happy when nothing makes sense, when no moment connects to the next? The thread of her life is gone.

Like a researcher on a quest for a missing piece, I am consumed with trying to work out in my own mind the structure of this puzzle. I cannot sort out what is best for her. My gut reaction says tube feeding is inhumane because it denies her the taste of food. Taste is one of the few momentary pleasures she has left. Tube feeding is a way of eating she cannot understand. It might also cause her some pain. More importantly, forcing her to "eat" in this manner in order to sustain a life without a past or a future feels wrong. I know, without question, that if I get Alzheimer's, I do not want to be tube fed.

Two days after the conference, I am driving with some friends in a car. As we ride along, one of them tells a story about how her grandmother stayed alive long enough to see her mother one last time before she died. It is a moving and powerful story about the body's will to live for a connection to love and life. As she tells the story, I can visualize this woman's mother driving through the night to see her mother, coming into the room around dawn, taking her mother's hand, telling her she loves her, knowing full well that her presence will enable her mother to take her last breath and die peacefully.

Ironically, this story sums up our dilemma: our mother no longer has anyone to wait for because she doesn't know us anymore. Just as she has died already for us, we have died for her. We are gone from each other's lives, but we are still living in each other's worlds.

I feel pressed by the conference to look at new ways to make connections with my mother and for my mother with the world in general and the medical establishment specifically. This is really the task at hand.

I fear we are doing this business all wrong and need to rethink "treatment" and be more creative in our "medical management." We must spend both time and money to explore possible new pleasures and opportunities that are being missed for Alzheimer's victims and their families.

Alzheimer's claims many victims in its brushfire of destruction: family members are often as deeply burned as the patients themselves. Sometimes we wonder if we are the ones hurting, while Mom continues oblivious to her condition.

I understand that weight gain and weight loss are both

significant indicators of disease and disorder in a body. I also understand that there is more to Alzheimer's than body mass. Researchers need to talk with medical ethicists and with families in order to get a clear picture of what is at stake in the lives of all involved.

We also need to remember the stories of the promising medical student and young mother in order to shake ourselves free from the blinding concept that Alzheimer's is strictly a geriatric disease suitably treatable with a geriatric model.

14

THE BEGINNING OF THE END

My brother Chuck was the one to call. I was getting dinner ready when the phone rang. He was shaken but sounded calm. Mom had fallen and broken her hip. Despite the wheelchair, she had never quite understood that her right leg didn't work anymore and she was unable to walk. She'd taken a couple of spills before, trying to get out of her wheelchair, but other than a bruise or two, she hadn't hurt herself badly until now.

Chuck said he had talked to the Methodist Home, and Mom was on her way to St. Joseph's Hospital in Ann Arbor in an ambulance. I told him I'd call him back as soon as I could get a plane reservation.

It was too late to catch an evening flight, so I booked the first one out the next morning for Cole and me. I called Chuck to let him know that Cole and I would be coming in the morning, then called Lolly at work to let her know when we'd be arriving.

The next morning, Lolly picked us up at the airport. We dropped our two boys off at Colin's nursery school, then drove straight to the hospital. When we arrived a little after ten A.M., Mom was in preop and the surgeon was waiting for us. There were papers to sign. In our haste and confusion, we had forgotten that Mom was no longer a consenting adult and that we would have to sign for her.

The nurse took us to see Mom. She was on a gurney with IVs running in the back of her hand. Pillows bolstered her right leg and hip. She was heavily sedated and didn't respond when we touched her or called out her name.

The nurse handed us a clipboard jammed with papers and told us to read them and sign in the appropriate places. She also told us the doctor would be over to see us directly and would discuss the operation with us. If we preferred, we could wait to sign until after we had talked to him.

There were many papers. The task was daunting, and the sudden escalation of responsibility was overwhelming. Lolly read through the first set of papers regarding the dangers of anesthesia and turned to me. The question was simple: What would Mom want?

It was *the* question that had rumbled and rolled around in the air for the past five years. We had all thought about what she would want when it came to life supports, tube feeding, surgery, and medical interventions of any kind.

Whenever we talked about it, we all agreed, above all else, that Mom was fiercely proud, and we knew without question she would want to go through both life and death with dignity.

But in the light of Alzheimer's, what does "life and death with dignity" really mean? Also, who Mom was before and who she is now are two different people. Even if the "old" Mom could by some miracle come back for an hour to help us make decisions for her, we weren't sure she would know what this "new" Mom would want.

The surgeon drew the curtain back and made a place for himself in our little circle and softly, clearly, laid out the options: (1) do nothing, (2) do a full hip replacement, or (3) pin the broken ball joint. We asked questions, and he answered. He was candid and straightforward. Doing nothing would involve a lot of medication, waiting, and lying still. A full hip replacement would have to be followed by intensive physical therapy. Pinning the broken hip joint would be the least invasive surgery and would give her, in time, the same mobility she had before and would require only limited physical therapy.

When he finished his talk and answered our questions, he paused briefly before going on. No matter what our decision, he warned us—and it was *our* decision as legal guardians—in his experience, when Alzheimer's victims suffered a physical trauma like a broken hip, they usually took some unexpected slide backward, losing some ability. It might be motor, it might be cognitive, he didn't know. But he wanted us to be aware that although he could fix the hip, in some way she would change. She would not be the same.

The Mom we knew was gone. The one who remained had become some rapidly flickering kaleidoscope of pieces falling and mating, scrambling and reassembling at random. Every day seemed to bring a new someone we didn't know any better than the last who had momentarily been in focus. The prospect of a dramatically diminished person now becoming "Mom" left us holding our breath.

"What do we do?" Lolly asked as the doctor stepped away to let us discuss the options. The doctor had carefully explained that they could do the full hip replacement only if Mom were capable of physical therapy. When we asked what that entailed, he asked if she could follow directions. We told him the truth: no. That option was gone.

So we were really down to two options: doing nothing and keeping her immobilized with medication until the hip could stabilize on its own, or doing the minimal surgery to pin the broken joint. Both of these options had their problems, but the bottom line was clear: we would be the ones to decide.

I thought I knew, when we made the decision to put Mom in the Methodist Home, what it was to make decisions for someone else. I thought my brothers and sister and I had felt the weight of that burden and had continued to shoulder the responsibility as she was moved from the Alzheimer's wing to the medical wing. Those early decisions, it turned out, were merely a warm-up, a little exercise in our growing responsibility for Mom.

Now we would have to decide whether she would have surgery or be confined to bed and kept immobile with drugs. In order to clarify our own thinking, Lolly and I talked again about our decision at the Methodist Home to have Mom declared a Code A—no tube feeding, life supports, or resuscitation. We were quite clear on this issue. Even though Mom never made a living will, she made it clear to us, long before she had Alzheimer's, that she did not want to be kept alive by any artificial means.

Would she want to be drugged and kept immobile in a bed in order to have her hip heal? Probably not. So we made the only decision we thought reflected her wishes: to have her hip pinned.

When we talked to the doctor, giving him our decision, we explained her Code A status and reviewed her history of Alzheimer's. He drew pictures of the surgical procedure and took time to answer more questions. Then before he left, he told us he thought we had made the most humane decision, the same decision he would have made if she were his mother.

It took Mom a long time to come around after the surgery. Her breathing was erratic and labored, and her blood pressure danced all around. We stayed with her until late in the evening when she, at last, stabilized.

The next morning she had a fever and the threat of pneumonia. Her blood count and blood pressure were dropping, so we had to sign more papers authorizing antibiotics and a couple of units of blood.

She was extremely agitated and went in and out of sleep, talking in both states of consciousness in a jumbled, crazy way, punctuated by shouts and threatening swipes of her hand. The staff informed us we were to let them know whenever we left so they could put her in a straitjacket in order to keep her from pulling out her IVs.

The IVs were a problem. They bothered her. Other things agitated her as well: the parade of nurses, the blood pressure and temperature checks, and the long plastic inflatable cuffs on her legs that alternately pumped up and released first one leg then the other in order to prevent blood clots from forming in her legs. It was impossible to explain to her why these cuffs were there and what they did for her. Whenever she pulled at them and we moved her hands away and attempted once again to tell her they had to stay, she would shake her finger at us and shout, "No, no, no, you, you, you, don't."

Keeping her hands away from the IVs and the cuffs was exhausting. It was easier, however, to manage psychologically than having her constrained in a straitjacket.

We stayed with her for four days and on into the nights, when she at last would fall into a deep, deep sleep. One day Colin and Cole came with me to the hospital while Lolly went to work. Another day just Cole came. The boys were a good distraction, although occasionally for no explainable reason she would start to shout at them, "No, no, no, you, you, you, don't."

When she slept, she would have long disjointed conversations while her arms waved and reached out. During these times, I began to wonder if there were spirits in the room.

One evening, waiting for her to fall into a peaceful state of sleep, I found myself wishing my mother's sister Aunt Alice, her favorite of all her siblings, would come to visit her. Alice had died a couple of years before from cancer, and it seemed to me as though she was talking to Alice in these animated sleep conversations. Maybe she was.

One morning when I came to stay with Mom, a rather curt physical therapist informed me I had to leave because she was getting Mom up for a walk. When I asked her who was going to help her, she put her hands on her hips and informed me she didn't need anyone to help her.

I stood there dumbfounded. Mom hadn't walked for almost a year by then. She was also both big and strong and had a history of fighting with anyone who tried to move her physically.

"Did you see the chart?" I asked her. "Mom has Alzheimer's."

"Of course, but she can still walk."

"Who said?" I asked, this time getting a little annoyed.

"She did."

I was sure Mom did, because if anyone asked her anything, she would either say yes or no depending on her mood. At about this point in our conversation, the therapist pulled my mother's shoulders up from the bed in an attempt to sit her up. My mother started shouting, "No, no, no, you, you, you, no, no, no." Her voice was firm and commanding, and the fight in her eyes flashed wildly enough for the therapist to reconsider her intentions and ease Mom back down onto her pillows. The therapist then turned and left the room, mumbling something about a person ought to know well enough if she can walk or not. The therapist never came back.

A couple of weeks before the fall that broke her hip, Mom had had a fight with a gentleman on the ward. The staff was never able to discern what provoked the fight, but in the end, Mom and the man got in a tussle over his cane, and they both wound up on the floor. Mom suffered a bad bruise on her head, and her glasses got broken. The man was a little bruised as well. Overall, Mom was very combative, and it was not always possible to anticipate when she might feel like fighting. There were some times, however, when she would warn you.

One morning when I came to stay with her, she was very angry. The IVs had been in for three days by then and must have been very uncomfortable. When I walked into the room, she turned her head away from me, then started yelling, "No, no, no, you, you, *you.*"

Then she held out the hand with the IV. When I moved forward to touch her, I began talking quietly about not being able to take out the IVs. This made her very agitated. She pulled her hand back and tried to pull the needle out on her own, so I gently but quickly took both of her hands in mine and held them.

She calmed, then dropped her hands to her sides and started mumbling something that sounded distinctly like "Slap you, slap you."

This seemed to me like a fair enough warning, so I let go and backed off. Just as I was backing away, the new shift nurse came in. I had never met her before and introduced myself. She was one of those lovely but a-little-too-bubbly ladies in white.

"These Alzheimer's people are the sweetest old things," she gushed. And before I could stop her, she bent down over my mother's head to kiss her.

I could hear the pitch of my mother's voice rise as the woman moved closer to her, the cadence "slap you, slap you" building steam. I could see what was going to happen. I had seen my mother hit a nurse before. I had no desire to witness it again, so I calmly told her to move back.

"Listen," I said, "she's saying she's going to slap you. Move back. She will. She's going to slap you."

It was an incredible relief to have Mom moved back to the Methodist Home where people knew her and respected her little idiosyncrasies. It was a relief to have the IVs gone and the pumping machine pulled off, as well as all the decision making over with for a while.

As the doctor predicted, Mom did decline. Over the next couple of months following the surgery, she began to lose more language. By Christmas she had only twenty or thirty words left. *No, yes, you, now, good, boy, need, don't, okay* are the ones that ring in my head.

In addition, no matter how hard the physical therapist at the Methodist Home would try, Mom refused to move her hurt leg. She would also, from time to time, start to cry and say the word *hurt*.

To make matters much more complicated, she developed a fighting-mad phobia about being taken off the ward. It made sense to me. The last time they took her away, she went to a place that hurt her, kept her tied down, and poked her all the time. This fear of being taken away from the ward was an odd reassurance. It let us know Mom still made real-life connections in her mind. This new development complicated our lives and the staff's a little, but it let us know "Mom" was still there.

Unfortunately, Mom had to be taken back to St. Joseph's for X rays a couple of weeks later as a follow-up to the surgery. Lolly accompanied her. It took nearly four attendants to move Mom and keep her from hurting herself and an additional corps of hospital personnel to get the X rays. Lolly said it was an amazing three-hour battle. She was exhausted when she finally got Mom back to the Methodist Home.

By the time Christmas came around, I realized I too had reached a new plateau with the Alzheimer's: I was emotionally drained. I couldn't seem to get focused and get Christmas brewing at home. Lolly, however, was doing better. Between us there seemed to be only so much energy. Given that she was the one with the most pressing and immediate responsibility for Mom's care, I was glad she was rolling high.

Once again we had reservations for the train to go to Michigan for Christmas. If nothing else, Alzheimer's had introduced us to train travel. The slow, leisurely, enforced relaxation of the train was wonderful for all of us. For the children, it was an adventure punctuated by dinner in the dining car and a late-night movie in the observation car while the train rolled through the illuminated Christmas backyards of Virginia, Pennsylvania, and Ohio. For me, it was the time to read, relax, and adjust to the reality that the Mom I was going to see would again be different from the last.

Flying was too abrupt, too sudden of a movement from here to there: from the sanity of our home to the craziness of Mom and the Methodist Home. The car was a kind of cramped torture where someone always had to be awake to drive, and stopping for anything—a Coke, the bathroom, or dinner—meant just that much more time on the road.

As I was packing up the Christmas presents two days before we were to leave, Hedy discovered there were no packages for Mom. I hadn't been able to force myself to buy her anything. Nothing made sense. She couldn't read or write anymore. All her meals were provided. She had lots of clothes. She had a room with a bed, a chair, and a dresser. The Methodist Home provided everything else she needed. Whenever we bought her something fancy like hand lotion, it quickly disappeared and was replaced by one prescribed by her doctor. Also, the last time we brought her a present, it was a disaster. She wouldn't take it at first, then became upset and angry when one of the kids started unwrapping it for her. In the end, she kept the ribbon the package had been tied in and gave us back the gift.

In Hedy's clearly chiseled world of right and good, going to visit Grandma at Christmas without taking her a gift was out of the question. It made no sense to try to explain to Hedy that Grandma, my *real* mom who loved presents, was gone. The only real Grandma Hedy had known was the one we were going to visit.

"What should we get her?" I asked.

Getting wasn't good enough. Hedy decided we should make her a doll, a soft doll, because Grandma loved dolls.

Hedy took charge. Together we created a rag doll of sorts with an embroidered face and buttons for eyes. We made it from unbleached muslin. It looked a lot like a large, soft, unbaked gingerbread cookie. Hedy added short, knotted gray yarn for hair, and we found a dress in our stash of doll clothes. I embroidered Mom's name on the back of the doll so the staff would know it was hers.

We decided not to wrap it, given our most recent gift-giving fiasco. We brought it unwrapped to Mom on Christmas Day. When Hedy held it out to her, Mom's face lit up, and she took it. She kissed the doll and cooed, rubbing it against her cheek. "I like," she said, "I like her."

For the next few days, she always had the doll in her arms when we visited her. One day, however, when Hedy and I went alone to see Mom, she didn't have the doll with her. It was sitting on her chair in her room.

Hedy picked the doll up and walked over to Mom to give it to her. Without any warning, Mom took the doll with one hand and swung at Hedy with the other. She hit Hedy, a square sure body blow, but didn't knock her down. Tears welled up in Hedy's eyes. She was hurt both inside and out.

What do you say? Mom didn't mean to do it. She really loves you. I know, Hedy, she loves you. Maybe she thought you were trying to take the doll. She loves the doll. She loves you, Hedy, I know she loves you.

15

WE HAVE SO
MUCH TO LEARN
FROM EACH OTHER

I have been asked to speak about my family's experiences with Alzheimer's. The room is hot and crowded. They had thought twenty people might show up. There are forty, maybe fifty. They've had to get more chairs. The staff is standing at the back of the room. The overhead is hot and noisy.

This is the sixth or seventh talk I've given in as many weeks. Sometimes I worry I will forget what I'm supposed to say. I never do, but I imagine I could. Anyone could under the circumstances, but this fear of forgetting puts an edge on things. Every time I forget something, I worry I might be getting Alzheimer's.

I look out over the room and make a mental note of how many men have come. It's an unconscious thing I do each time before I speak. I don't need research to tell me that women are the primary caregivers. Whenever I speak about Alzheimer's, the room is filled with daughters, daughters-in-law, and wives. The sisters always sit together, their heads touching at times, nodding, comparing notes. They invariably raise their hands and ask what they are to do about the brother or the other sister who refuses to accept what is happening or help them take responsibility. The wives ask questions about drugs they've read about: miracle cures. They are the ones who cry.

I notice a woman in the third row. She is distracted and fidgeting. She is wearing a beautiful silk skirt that she is pleating with her fingers. She folds the material in her hands, then lets it go. Folds it, then lets it go. Sometimes when she lets it go, she stops for a minute and picks lint from the sleeve of her sweater. I try to make eye contact but fail. I am not a doctor, but I have learned to recognize the twitchy obsessive-compulsive behaviors you see so often in Alzheimer's patients.

There is an elegant man in a wheelchair sitting next to her. He has the most beautiful face. It is nut brown and smooth, with deep lines at his eyes and mouth. His face is a map of a lifetime of living and caring. He smiles at me and nods his head. He knows what I've seen.

When I finish my talk, he raises his hand. He cannot raise it very high. I can tell by the way that he moves his body that he has had a stroke. It takes him a moment or two to speak. His words come slowly. I make eye contact with him so he will know I am listening to him and that I have all the time in the world to hear what he has to say. I will not let anyone interrupt him.

"What," he says, making a slight nod to his wife, "can one do, once you know for sure, to make the lives of these people more beautiful?"

I have to catch my breath to keep from crying. More beautiful. What can we do to make the lives of these people more beautiful? I take my time searching my mind for an answer. I have no answer. I don't know why, but the first thing I think about is the short story by Hemingway, "A Clean, Well-Lighted Place."

There is an old man in the story. He is deaf and alone. It is rumored that last week he tried to commit suicide. Each night he comes to sit in the restaurant to drink. He likes to come in the evening because in the daytime the street is dusty, but at night the dew settles the dust, and he can feel the difference and the quiet.

There are two waiters in the restaurant. One is young and married. The other is older and has no family. It is late and near closing time. The young waiter is impatient to go home to his wife. He is annoyed with the old man. He doesn't understand why he can't drink at home and why he has to come every night and to sit alone drinking until past closing time.

The old man asks for another drink, and the younger waiter refuses, telling him he is finished, that he is drunk already. The old man stands up with dignity and pays his bill. He leaves a tip, then walks down the street alone.

The older waiter does not understand why the younger waiter wouldn't let the old man stay. As he argues with the younger man, it becomes clear to him that drinking alone at home is not the same as being able to come to a clean, well-lighted place to drink. He tells the younger waiter who is in a hurry to get home to his family that they shouldn't have closed the restaurant and sent the man home. He realizes that he is like the old man, because he too likes to stay late at the café. He tells the other waiter, "I am of those who like to stay late at the café . . . all those who do not want to go to bed . . . all those who need a light for the night."

More beautiful. I tell the man who asked the question that I believe we all need a clean, well-lighted place. When we take care of someone who has Alzheimer's, we bear the responsibility of finding the "clean, well-lighted place" and of keeping them safe.

I am forced by his question to think about what pleasure and happiness there is in life when there is no memory. I realize that we are connected to each other and therefore to the earth by memory. We are also connected by our senses of sight, touch, taste, and smell. I come to realize that in our scramble to try to make things better, to "fix" what's wrong with Alzheimer's, we have forgotten about the things that haven't been hurt. We have been so obsessed with the loss of memory, of all the memories, that we have forgotten to pay attention to what is left once the memories are gone.

What can we do to make these lives more beautiful?

We can touch. We can hold hands and hug. We can kiss and caress. We can comb hair and rub on lotion. We can make sure the blankets are smooth and soft. We can provide the best we have. Just as we would for a child.

As Alzheimer's progresses, its victims become more and more childlike. Think of your children. Think of a small child, a baby. Would you wrap them in a rough blanket? Would you let them get cold? Would you let them eat bad food?

Food and shelter are fundamental. They can also provide pleasure. And pleasure is something we need to focus on once the memories are gone. Because once the past has disappeared, the momentary pleasures are all that remain.

One of the primary and surely universal pleasures of life is food. Unfortunately, in a medical setting, where many Alzheimer's patients find themselves in their last years, food is often treated like a controlled substance: one serving of fruit, one of leafy greens, one protein, one starch, all to be served with eight ounces of liquid, none of which should be high fat, high salt, or high sugar.

Shortly after the evening when the gentleman asked how to make the lives of these people more beautiful, I was in Michigan visiting my sister and my mother. I also attended a care conference for my mother. During the care conference, the head nurse introduced my sister and me to the dietitian, and then she told us that our mother had gained some weight over the last eighteen months, so the doctor put her on a 1,600-calorie diet. I was speechless. I thought my sister was going to rise out of her chair and hit someone. A 1,600-calorie diet? What was that doctor thinking about? Surely he wasn't thinking about my mother, about her condition, about her life. He must have been thinking simply about her body. But we are all more than just our bodies. Aren't we?

I smiled. I composed myself. Then I began to lecture. I talked about how important it was that my mother have food that tastes good. Food she likes. I told them she has always loved desserts, that a diet was the wrong thing for her at this point in her life. I commented that I believed my mother didn't care about the size of her thighs any more than we did. That we were her guardians, her family, and we didn't have plans for her to enter some beauty contest. Instead, we wanted her to have the best of what there was for the rest of her life. We wanted her to have dessert.

Quality of life is a real issue with Alzheimer's, an issue its victims can't discuss. As caregivers, we need to take the responsibility on this issue, just as we would if we were the parents of a dying child.

I can't understand or share the physician's concern about my mother's weight. The next day I visited my mother in the afternoon and took her off her wing to the soda shop in the independent living area of the complex. There I bought her a hot fudge sundae. After the first spoonful, her face became animated. She made some noises, some loud noises. I spooned in more. She tilted her head my way and opened her mouth. She doesn't smile anymore, but it was clear she was pleased. It took all of my attention to keep feeding her and fending off her hands. It was a bit of a struggle to keep her from grabbing at the spoon and slinging hot fudge everywhere, but we managed. In between bits of ice cream, I was giving her sips of water because I know how thirsty ice cream can make you. I was drinking a Coke. At one point, when I tried to give her water, she shook her head. The next time I took a sip of Coke, she tried to grab my drink, so I let her have a sip. Her eyes opened wide, and she made a long, loud noise that sounded just like what you imagine those Campbell's Soup twins must sound like when then say *mmmmmmmm, mmmmmmmmmmm good.*

Was the hot fudge sundae good for her body? Maybe not. Was it good for her spirit, for her soul, for the precious untouchable piece of her that is tied to the moment? Yes. Was it good for me to feed her that hot fudge sundae? Yes. In this simple way, I could bring her a momentary pleasure, a respite from her disease.

There is much to learn from this. We must be the guardians of the moment for these people we love. We must be diligent to be sure they are getting not only what they need medically but also what might bring them some pleasure. We need to "think out of the box" a little. We need to push aside our concerns over the loss of memory, the loss of function. We need to be creative in our care. We need to find new ways to relate, to be in love with each other, and to focus on what is left, not what is lost.

We also need to learn to take a break from this caregiving, just as we take breaks from parenting and get a baby-sitter so we can "go out" with our spouses. So many times what I see in the caregivers who come to my talks is wonderful people who have given selflessly, who have given their all, and who are worn thin. If I were a pediatrician and saw these same caregivers in my office with a sick child, I would give them a prescription for their child, then urge them to hire a baby-sitter for an evening. I would tell them they need a break in order to be good parents. I would tell them their child needs them to be there for them, but also to be rested and happy.

From onset to death with Alzheimer's is, on average, seventeen years. A childhood. A lifetime. If we are to be the caregivers we want to be, we need to have lives that are happy. We need to take breaks. We need to feed our own souls so we can guard those who are in our care.

We need to remember what love is all about. We need to honor the pleasures of living, of being alive and of caring. We need to think more about how we can make not only the lives of these people, but our own lives, more beautiful.

I am grateful that beautiful man came to hear me that evening. He gave me more than he will ever know.

16

THINGS YOU CAN
AND SHOULD DO

When You Begin to Suspect Something
May Be Wrong

It's important to remember that the early stages of Alzheimer's are difficult for both family members and physicians to recognize. There are no physical presenting symptoms, no fever, headaches, backaches, bruises, growths, shortness of breath, or anything anyone can see or point to and say, "Look at this—there must be something wrong."

Instead, there are forgotten appointments, unexplained explosions of anger, forgetfulness, confusion, and changes in behavior.

Although not every Alzheimer's victim displays all the characteristics of Alzheimer's, most of them show one or more of the following:

- *Changes in eating patterns.* Someone with short-term memory loss often cannot remember if or when they've eaten and may overeat or fail to eat enough. Therefore you may see either a weight gain or a weight loss. Also, many Alzheimer's victims develop a craving for sweets during the early stages of the disease. You might see them eating two desserts, eating nothing but sweets, or buying and hoarding candy bars.

- *Changes in personal hygiene.* Alzheimer's victims will often forget to take care of personal hygiene, or they might become confused as to how to do it correctly. They may quit bathing, brushing their teeth, and/or changing into fresh clothing in the morning. They may also wear inappropriate clothing, like a bathrobe instead of a coat, or a sweater under a blouse, or their underwear over their outer clothing.

  They may also have trouble with using the toilet. They may not wipe themselves properly after a bowel movement, or they may forget or refuse to flush the toilet.

  Many Alzheimer's victims who are living on their own "forget" to wash their clothes, or how to wash their clothes, so they wear the same clothes over and over again.

- *Concerns about finances.* Many Alzheimer's victims become obsessed with financial matters. They may express concerns about having enough money to live on. They may also worry that someone is trying to steal their money.

  Many Alzheimer's victims are also confused about

money. They may forget how to write out a check. They may open their bills, throw the bills away, and keep the envelopes. Or, they may just "forget" to pay their bills.

They may also become confused and agitated when trying to pay for an item in a store. They may not know what denomination of bill to give a cashier to pay for an item, or they may become angry when the cashier tries to give them back change.

- *Changes in sleep patterns.* Many Alzheimer's victims begin to have difficulty sleeping during the night. And/or they may fall asleep in the afternoon or mid-morning. They may develop a sleeping pattern where they sleep for three to four hours, then are up for a couple of hours nervously pacing around, then sleep again, then pace some more.

  When they sleep like this, they often wake up in the middle of the night not knowing where they are or who you are or what they are supposed to be doing.

  They may also wander at night during this "pacing" time, going outside of the house and getting lost.

- *Changes in personality.* Many Alzheimer's victims begin to exhibit changes in personality during the early stages. What many family members report is a heightening or intensification of lifelong personality traits, as if some restraint on that trait has now been lifted. For instance, someone who has always been a little bit of a gossip now talks about everyone all the time, even in front of the person they are gossiping about. Someone who has been generous starts giving everything away to anyone who comes to the door. Someone who has been a bit mean-spirited becomes cruel. Someone who has been outspoken becomes hypercritical.

Many Alzheimer's victims become hypercritical of family members and friends. They may make unreasonable demands, or they may interpret how people react to them in ways that seem paranoid or out of line.

Unfortunately, few of these "symptoms" get played out in the doctor's office. So without your help, the doctor is forced to fall back to his or her normal routine of checking for physical symptoms that might point to trouble.

If you suspect your loved one might have Alzheimer's, keep a diary for a couple of weeks noting unusual behaviors or behaviors that might indicate short- or long-term memory loss. Be brief but specific in your diary. If you suspect something is wrong with your mother because she did not come to your birthday party, give the doctor a brief description of why this is out of the ordinary. For example, you could say, "I called my mother at the beginning of the week to invite her to our house for dinner on Friday to celebrate my birthday. When she didn't show up, I called her to remind her and ask her if she wanted my husband to come pick her up. She got angry with me and told me I had failed to ask her to come. When I tried to tell her I had invited her, she got mad and hung up the phone."

Everyone forgets an appointment or invitation. But forgetting they had been invited or getting angry when they are reminded is something a doctor should know about your loved one. It is the kind of behavior you see in Alzheimer's victims in the early stages. You want to note any behavior, response, or memory loss that seems unusual to you in your diary in order to present a "whole" picture.

Make a copy of these notes to give to the doctor. If you see a pattern of behavior developing, note that pattern in the margin. Then mail your notes to the doctor with a brief letter outlining your concerns and giving the day and time of your upcoming appointment. Or if you want, take the notes with you when you go to the appointment, and give them to the doctor. The more behavioral information your doctor has, the better he or she will be able to know how to proceed in diagnosing the problem.

Before you begin to talk to your doctor about the possibility of Alzheimer's, please be sure your loved one has had a full physical. A number of other illnesses present just like Alzheimer's, and they need to be ruled out first. These include Parkinson's disease, depression, vitamin B_{12} deficiency, and a series of small strokes.

If your doctor does not take your concerns seriously, or if you feel, for whatever reasons, that you can't talk to him or her about what you are experiencing, find another doctor.

Once a full physical is completed and everything else except Alzheimer's has been ruled out, you will want to get an appointment with a neurologist. Neurologists are trained to test a wide range of neurological disorders, including the loss of short- and long-term memory.

During this time of testing and evaluating, continue to keep the behavioral diary. These notes will be helpful to the neurologist in making his or her diagnosis.

Taking Charge

Since most families have some unresolved sibling issues of control and authority, it is important to get the family together to discuss the diagnosis of Alzheimer's and what it will mean for everyone involved.

There is much to discuss. First, Alzheimer's is a terminal illness. Second, there is, at present, no miracle cure. Third, on average, from onset to death with Alzheimer's takes seventeen years.

If your family is like most families, by the time you have come to suspect something is wrong, you have probably lived through three to five years of denial of the disease. This still leaves about twelve years of care ahead of you. But since the "average" is seventeen years, you could be looking at fewer years of care, or you could be looking at more.

Someone needs to take the role of primary caregiver. Who will that be in your family? Also, where will the person be cared for? In their own home, in the family member's home, or in an assisted living unit?

Caring for someone with Alzheimer's is a twenty-four-hour-a-day job. You need to know that and to discuss what it means for you and your family.

Caring for an Alzheimer's victim can be rewarding. It can also be frustrating and stressful. The primary caregiver is going to need help from all the members of the family. This help might be financial, physical, or emotional. More than likely, it will be all three.

The most important thing you can do during these early stages and early decision times is to agree that each of you has a responsibility and a desire to help with the care of your loved one. Do not be surprised or discouraged if one of your family members disagrees with the doctor's diagnosis and prognosis. Alzheimer's is a scary disease, and no one wants to believe that someone they love has it.

Unfortunately, you may discover that the person who has agreed to take responsibility as the primary caregiver may not be the person whom the Alzheimer's victim responds to the best. In fact, many Alzheimer's victims are unable to recognize the person who becomes the primary caregiver as a family member or for that matter as someone whom they know. It's just one of those odd things about Alzheimer's.

If this is the case in your family, as it was in ours, you

may find that you need to identify a "point man" as well as a primary caregiver. The point man plays an essential role during the early stages of the disease. This is the time when you have to make a lot of decisions and changes in living arrangements.

Our point man was our younger brother, Chuck. He was the only one of us whom Mom believed was her child. So he was the only one she trusted. Without his cooperation and the role he played in introducing her to the idea of moving and giving up her home, we would not have been able to get her into a safe place.

If you find you're meeting with a lot of resistance from family members regarding the diagnosis and the need for someone to take charge of caregiving, ask them to talk with the doctor. Or better yet, have them spend a long weekend with the family member in question. It usually doesn't take more than a day or two for people to be convinced not only that something is wrong but that someone needs to do something about it.

The Car

Whether you have decided to care for your family member at their home, your own home, or an assisted living unit, once you have determined with your doctor that they have some form of dementia, you have to deal with the car.

This is one of the most difficult issues in the early and middle stages of Alzheimer's. However alert you feel your loved one is, if they are exhibiting behaviors that indicate a loss of either short- or long-term memory, they are not capable of making quick judgments and should not be behind the wheel of a car.

Until very recently the medical profession viewed the early stages of Alzheimer's as rather benign. Consequently, there wasn't the sense that Alzheimer's victims shouldn't drive in those early stages. As we learn more and more about how this disease works in the brain, however, those ideas and attitudes are changing.

We now understand that even in the early stages, Alzheimer's victims are not capable of making quick judgments and/or physical responses and therefore shouldn't be driving—even if they insist they can still drive. When trying to muster the courage to take the car away, it is important to remind yourself how bad you would feel if your loved one were hurt or killed in an accident while driving, or if they hit and killed a child.

How do you take the car away? The Alzheimer's Association has asked physicians to write prescriptions for family members saying their loved one can no longer drive because they have dementia. As we all know, the prescription pad or the word of the doctor is very powerful.

I know of numerous families who have had the car "stolen." Usually the confusion of the "theft" and the act of having to go out and buy a new car (that is, test-driving cars with dealers riding with the Alzheimer's victim, having to pay for the car, and the like) puts an end to the desire to drive.

Some families have removed spark plugs or otherwise made the car inoperable. When the Alzheimer's victim discovers the car needs to be repaired and must be towed, it is easy to have the car towed away and just held at an auto repair shop indefinitely.

You can, of course, just say that you're taking their car away. But that is probably the hardest for the family to pull off and the most punishing for the Alzheimer's victim. Few Alzheimer's victims can be rational about such key decisions as driving, living on their own, and so on.

Probably the best and most face-saving way to remove a car is to tell the Alzheimer's victim you're thinking about buying a new car for yourself, your son, your daughter, or your nephew. Make a good case as to why they need the car (for work, for school, it's a better car than the one they've got, it's a safer car than the one they've got). Then ask if you could buy the car from them.

This provides a graceful out for the person with dementia. Often they'll make the car a gift and have an opportunity to feel like the adult in charge in this situation rather than the child. If they do not make the car a gift but rather offer to sell it, consider the money well spent.

Looking at the Long Range

Alzheimer's progresses over a long period of time, and as it develops, the needs of the Alzheimer's victim change.

As these needs change, the role of the caretaker changes as well.

Unlike other terminal illnesses such as cancer or heart disease, where there is a clear diagnosis followed by a treatment plan, Alzheimer's has no set "plan." There are no radiation treatments, diet changes, or exercise programs that will take the patient into good health or remission. Instead, there is a long slow decline of mental and physical functioning.

And just about the time you've managed to establish a care routine, the disease progresses a little bit more, and the needs and behaviors of the Alzheimer's victim no longer fit your plans.

The best thing you and your family can do for yourselves is to look ahead to what will happen next. This way you will not always be working out of crisis. Today you may be able to take care of the needs of your loved one by paying bills, buying groceries, and visiting them daily to make sure they're okay. Tomorrow you might need to bring them into your home so you can watch over them twenty-four hours a day. At some point early on, you'll have to take the car away, and when you do, you'll then have to provide transportation. In the not-so-distant future, you might need adult day care so you can get a break—or go to work. Also, you'll be better prepared to decide, when the time comes, whether to use outside assisted living if you already know what's available.

In other words, you need to know what services are

available to you and your family in your community, not only for your present needs but also for needs that may develop in the future. If you are trying to care for a loved one long distance, then you need to know what's available there and whether it would be advisable to move the Alzheimer's victim closer to you now or later.

Assisted Living Facilities

Visit the facilities you are considering. Talk to the staff. Learn to trust your instincts. If you walk into a facility that looks good but feels bad to you, it's probably not the place you want for your family member. If you're not comfortable there, you can be assured that they won't be comfortable there either.

There are a number of issues to consider when looking at facilities for Alzheimer's victims. The first issue is safety. Alzheimer's victims have a tendency to pace and wander. You want to be sure that whatever facility you send them to, whether for day care or for assisted living care, is managed in such a way that your loved one cannot wander off and get lost.

You should also look to see if the facility is clean and odor free. At some point, all Alzheimer's victims become incontinent. You want to be sure the residents are being changed and bathed frequently. If they are, you should be able to tell. If you have some concerns, ask the director about their personal hygiene policies, that is, how frequently clients are changed and bathed and what is done to prevent skin rashes.

When you ask questions, are the staff friendly and helpful? Have they been there a long time, or are most of them relatively new? Spend time at the facility, and watch how the staff interact with the clients. Do they talk to the Alzheimer's victims? Do they touch them? Do they call them by name and tell them what they are going to do with them (take them for a walk, feed them, change them, and so on)? Or do they just do their job without talking to the clients, as if they have lost not only their memories but also their ability to think, hear, see, and feel as well?

Find out if there is an emergency backup plan in case of disaster. How would the staff evacuate the building? What would they do if one of the Alzheimer's patients walked off?

You'll also want to know if the residents have activities and go on outings. You'll want to know what the staff-to-resident ratio is, both in the facility and when they are out. You should also ask how residents are transported.

Ask about the licensing of the agency and the qualifications of the staff. Are they trained in caring for Alzheimer's victims? Do they have ongoing staff-development programs? Do the staff members get enough breaks in their day to remain fresh at their jobs?

Ask about food preparation and mealtimes. Are the Alzheimer's victims encouraged to feed themselves—despite how messy it gets—or are they fed by the staff?

Are finger foods supplied so that, once they can no longer manage a fork or spoon, they can continue to have the independence of feeding themselves? What does the food look like? If it all looks gray and mushy to you, and therefore unappetizing, it will look gray and mushy to an Alzheimer's victim as well—and therefore quite unappetizing. Remember, once you have lost all your short- and long-term memory, the few pleasures you have left in this world are sight, taste, and touch. Food provides all three and therefore should be a major consideration in choosing a facility. The bottom line: mealtimes should be high pleasure times. There should also be special meals that celebrate life: birthday meals, holiday meals, picnics, and ice cream socials. Food should be fun and social as well as nutritious.

Does the agency in question return your phone calls promptly? Do they address your concerns in a professional manner? Are the rates competitive with other services in your area? What is covered by the "flat" rate, and what is extra? Are their services covered by your medical insurance? Is the facility qualified to receive third-party payment from Medicare or Medicaid? Once you have used all your financial resources, will this facility accept Medicare or Medicaid payment?

How does the agency structure their "payment" system? Some agencies demand that all assets be signed over to them, including the Alzheimer's victim's home, before they take on their care. This can be a good situation for you if your loved one has limited resources and the agency is both reputable and can assume full responsibility over the long range for your family member. It can be a bad situation if the estate is large. You need the advice of a good estate planner to help you make this decision and to review the agency's contract carefully.

Likewise, some agencies keep their clients on month-to-month contracts, giving the agency the option to withdraw service anytime they wish. Agencies are acutely aware that personalities change as Alzheimer's develops. And a month-to-month contract gives them the option of getting rid of a patient who becomes belligerent or exhibits more physical problems than they feel capable of handling. On the other hand, a month-to-month contract gives you the option to leave without financial penalty if you are dissatisfied or your circumstances change.

You need to find out if there is a waiting list or if rooms are available immediately. If there is a waiting list, you'll want to know how long you will have to wait in order to secure a place.

Be sure you know if the agency you're considering provides a continuum of care. In other words, will they be able to help you care for your loved one as the disease progresses, or will you be stuck having to look for another agency as your loved one's condition changes?

Depending upon your circumstances, you might also want to know if the agency provides multiple levels of care, such as companion rooms for spouses. You should also find out whether, if you needed to, you could pay to have an aide come into the facility to help with your family member's care.

Find out if there is an agency near you that provides respite care as well as full-service assisted living care. In some circumstances, respite care can give you just enough relief to make it possible for you to continue to care for your loved one at home. You'll need to know how much notice is required before booking a short-term respite care situation and also whether the facility sets a minimum or maximum number of days that you can have for respite care. Ask if they require a deposit and if so, how much. If for some reason your plans change and you no longer need the respite care, can you get a refund on your deposit?

You may find many of the answers to these questions in the brochures and written materials from the various agencies you are looking at, so read their materials carefully. Reading materials, however, will not give you the best sense of whether one facility is better than another for your needs. When at all possible, visit the various facilities and talk with the staff before making any decisions.

Legal Issues

As I'm sure you could see in our story, there are a number of legal issues involved in taking care of an Alzheimer's victim. First and foremost, you cannot just assume full legal and financial responsibility for someone. The person has to grant you that right, and usually this is done through a Power of Attorney. Regular Power of Attorney does not give you the right to make all legal, financial, and medical decisions for someone. But Durable Power of Attorney and, in some cases, Health Care Power of Attorney, will.

Since there are subtle differences from state to state regarding estates, it is important that you and your family get good legal advice. Find an attorney you both trust and can talk to. You need someone who is familiar with estate planning and wills. In addition, the lawyer should also be up to date and well informed on probate laws in your state.

Suppose you do not have either Power of Attorney or Durable Power of Attorney, and your loved one is confused or flat out refuses to grant you this power. (Remember, many Alzheimer's victims get concerned about money—and become concerned or convinced that someone is trying to steal their money, so your attempt to take "control" of that money may seem threatening.) In that case, you may have to go to court to get legal custody. Again, talk with an attorney so that you will understand your options and what you will have to do legally in order to take care of the person you love. As you take each step, either to secure Durable Power of Attorney or to gain legal custody, however, you should openly discuss what you are doing with each family member.

Legal and financial "things" within families are touchy. Depending upon how Alzheimer's progresses in your loved one, you may find that you have to spend the bulk of that person's estate in order to provide them with care. Remember that the prognosis for Alzheimer's from onset to death averages seventeen years. Even if you are able to provide care within your home for half of those years, that leaves eight or more years of care to be paid for out of pocket. Good assisted living care is expensive, and standard medical insurance does not cover it as yet. This means that the entire cost of the care will be yours to pay.

New insurance policies are coming along that are specifically for third-party payment of assisted living care for dementia patients. These are policies that individuals take out on themselves, like other additional medical insurance policies. Many of these policies are expensive and provide limited coverage. Read the fine print carefully, and consider having a lawyer review a policy before you commit to it.

Currently, Medicaid does not "kick in" until all one's personal assets have been spent down to less than $2,000. (This is a "round" number; the specific figure varies from state to state, but all states are within a couple hundred dollars of this figure.) "Personal assets" include all savings, stocks, bonds, and property. This includes the family home, which for many people is their largest asset.

In addition, in some circumstances Medicare does not cover the costs of assisted living. A local Medicare/

Medicaid representative can help you sort through what it will or will not cover in your situation.

It is important that every family member understand the full financial picture. In our own family, putting our mother into assisted living clearly meant that in the end there would likely be no estate. Also, it is illegal for someone who has been diagnosed with a terminal illness to transfer property in order to qualify for Medicaid. Since rules covering the transfer of property vary from state to state and also get changed from time to time, it is important to talk to a lawyer before you do anything.

Money

Before you panic over the cost of care and how you're going to pay for it all, talk with a good financial planner. They will be able to help you sort through your working assets and advise you on how to best use this money to pay for the care. Mom had a few CDs and some savings, but that was it. She also had a small house in a good section of town. After renting her home for about five years to make the most of the funds it could provide us, we sold it.

It's important to understand all your options: renting versus selling, long-term, high-yield CDs versus short-term, low-yield CDs, money market investments, and stocks. This is something, however, that's best done with professional advice.

If you have legal custody, you will have to provide the

courts with your books once a year to show how you have managed your loved one's financial affairs and how you have paid for all their bills. If you don't have legal custody but instead have Durable Power of Attorney, you should keep a clear accounting of how you have spent the estate money in order to finance your family member's care.

Taking Care of the Caregiver

No matter who is in charge and no matter how you slice it, those family members who live close to the Alzheimer's victims are the ones who do the greatest caregiving. They are able to visit more frequently. They can run errands and attend care conferences. And if the Alzheimer's victim is in assisted living, they are the ones the staff can call when things go wrong.

If you have a situation where one parent is deceased and only siblings are left to care for the parent who has Alzheimer's, be aware of your role as either a long- or short-distance sibling. If you are not the primary caregiver but you live close to the one who is, schedule a regular time where you can take charge and they can take time off. Do it as often as possible. This disease has a long slow course. You will need to provide quality care for a long time.

At least twice a year, send the primary caregiver on a vacation. If their circumstances do not allow them to get away, offer to take charge on weekends so they can get away mentally if not physically. Insist they do something once a week for themselves. It doesn't really matter what it is, as long as it gets them away from their caretaking job. It can be getting a manicure, bowling in a league, taking a class, or just having lunch with a friend. Such times will help them continue to provide the loving level of care they want and need to provide to the Alzheimer's victim.

You need to be honest about being a long-distance sibling versus a short-distance sibling. If you're a long-distance one, you need to be doubly aware of the stress and strain on the family members who are short-distance people.

All family members need to be aware that if a spouse is the primary caregiver, that person needs a tremendous amount of support. You can't just assume that Mom is taking care of Dad just as she always has and that you just need to remember to call her every week and send her flowers for her birthday.

Research and anecdotal observations show that when spouses are the caregivers, they are less likely than other caregivers to report abusive behavior from the Alzheimer's victim. Why? Because they are scared and also ashamed of what is happening. They feel somehow that their love has failed to fix what is broken. They're also afraid to report that they can't handle the situation because it might indicate that something is wrong with them as well.

It is not okay for your seventy-plus-years-old mother to be in charge of your father who has Alzheimer's. That is too much responsibility for a person of that age. If nothing else, because Alzheimer's victims often exhibit poor sleeping habits, this caregiver is not getting enough sleep, and her health can become endangered as well. Quite plainly, she is not physically capable of handling the situation. If the couple want to stay together, you need to help them by providing someone to come in during the day and sometimes during the night.

Many agencies have provisions for husbands and wives to stay together in their facilities. Sometimes they stay on the same floor in the same room. Other times, as the disease progresses and the Alzheimer's victim becomes more disoriented and more difficult, they are able to place the spouse in an appropriate room of their own where they can come to stay with the Alzheimer's victim anytime they want.

As a family, take time together away from the Alzheimer's illness to make new memories whenever you can. It is easy to have your whole life consumed by this disease. If you let it, you will become embittered over your own "loss of life."

Be aware of the physical and emotional stress that this disease imposes on the lives of all the family members involved. Each of us takes on the burden and guilt of this disease in different ways. No matter what your role in caregiving, try to find ways to release the stress you feel.

Get some exercise. Eat right. Take time for yourself and your own family, and whenever you can, remember the good times you had. Try not to dwell on all that has been lost. Instead, think of all you've had together as a family, and celebrate that.

POSTSCRIPT

How do you end a book like this? The obvious answer seems to be: with my mother's death. But I have chosen to end with my mother's life still intact. I have made a conscious decision to not "wrap the package" with a neat ribbon, a tight ending. Because the "end" of Alzheimer's is as ragged and elusive as the various "stages."

It feels like my mother will live forever, and we will be wrestling forever with her disease, her inch-by-inch destruction. It feels never-ending. It feels without hope.

Although she does not remember who we are or that we come to visit her, we continue to go to Michigan to see her. My children are able to brace themselves for the visits. They sit with her, hold her hand, push her in her wheelchair down the halls of the Methodist Home, and try to talk to her. My two nephews, who live in Chelsea and feel her presence daily, no longer like or want to visit with her. Lolly does the best she can for Mom, but she limits her time with her because it is just too hard to see her mother make animal-like noises, swipe at her with the back of her hand, and scream "No, no, no."

One day during a recent trip to Michigan, nothing anyone said or did seemed to calm Mom. She was agitated and verbal, alternately screaming at me and growling. My sister had described this new behavior to me beforehand, adding that she felt it made visiting Mom incredibly difficult. I listened patiently to Lolly's description and told her that I knew it must be hard but she needed to remember that Mom didn't mean anything by what she said or did anymore.

Fortunately, Lolly had opted to stay at home that day while I went to visit, so I wasn't forced to eat my well-intended words. You can rationalize that your mother is sick and doesn't mean what she says or does, but when she does it to you, it is hard to accept. I left in tears.

During the Ninth Annual Joseph and Kathleen Bryan Alzheimer's Disease Research Center Conference, one presenter flashed a graph on the screen and with his pointer showed us how, if you extend the graph of life expectancy, you see the statistical chance of getting Alzheimer's moves closer and closer to one hundred percent. In brief, his research showed that getting Alzheimer's is not really a question of *whether* but of *when*. In his opinion, if we live long enough, we will all, at the end of our lives, live without a past or a future. We will live without memory.

It is a sobering thought.

INDEX

Index

Index

Index

ABOUT THE AUTHOR

Carrie Knowles is an award-winning freelance writer. Her essays, articles, and short stories have appeared in numerous magazines and newspapers. Knowles has won many honors and awards for her writing, including an American Heart Association award for a three-part magazine series on cholesterol. In 1994 she received a North Carolina Arts Council Literary Nonfiction Writer's Grant to write *Alzheimer's: The Last Childhood*.

She lives in Raleigh, North Carolina, with her husband and their three children.